Ripley's ®

WHALES and Dolphins

Written by:
Doug Perrine

with an Introduction by:
Joseph M. Choromanski

Original Art by:
Corena Ricks

Series Edited by:
Edward Meyer

SCHOLASTIC INC.

New York Toronto London Auckland Sydney
Mexico City New Delhi Hong Kong Buenos Aires

Humpback whales can jump higher than any other animal on Earth and are often seen playfully leaping clear out of the water.

The Blue whale has a mouth so large several people could stand in it at the same time.

One of Ripley's very first whale cartoon facts, originally published in 1930, concerned a rare two-headed rorqual whale caught off the South Georgia Islands, near Antarctica.

Whales and Dolphins was designed by Infinite Ideas & Designs, Casselberry, Florida.

ISBN 0-439-34273-2

12 11 10 9 8 7 6 5 4 3 2   3 4 5 6/0

Printed in the U.S.A.

First Scholastic printing, October 2001

For over 70 years Ripley's Believe It or Not! has examined the fascinating world beneath the seas, publishing hundreds of unbelievable—but true—facts about marine life. Our founder, Robert Ripley was deeply intrigued by all the ocean's mysteries, and throughout his career, published several memorable cartoons about the largest of all marine life—whales.

Ripley's fourth whale cartoon, first published May 2, 1930, and redrawn in this volume by Corena Ricks (see facing page), concerned a rare two-headed whale. To this day this is the only reported case of this phenomena. Another of his early cartoons asked the question: What animal can jump the highest? Ripley was so sure no one would know the answer to this question that he offered autographed books to anyone who sent him the right answer. The correct answer of course is the whale, but Ripley was right; very few of his readers knew this fact. Likewise, his readers were astonished to learn that Humpback whales could sing; yet they do not have any vocal cords.

It is uncertain whether Ripley ever saw any whales in the wild. We do know, however, that he interacted with dolphins on a radio broadcast live from the world's first Oceanarium in St. Augustine, Florida. The Ripley archive photos show him assisting in a dolphin rescue, and the surviving audio describes his awe at their friendliness and intelligence as they ate fish from his hands on the tank's floor.

We also know that this experience had a profound effect on Ripley. He learned to respect these gentle giants and for the remainder of his life he taught the concepts of animal husbandry and conservation. Soon after his dolphin experience, Ripley reported and publicly admonished the existence of the last remaining whaling station in the United States.

Today scientists and students alike know a great deal more about whales, dolphins and porpoises than Ripley or his readers did. Through the study of these mysterious, magnificent, creatures, both in the wild and at aquariums, we have learned that they are highly intelligent, they can communicate, they are very social and they are almost never the feared monsters that have been depicted in literature and history. The fictional Moby Dick may have been a malevolent leviathan, but his kin, Keiko, the real life Killer whale of *Free Willy* movie fame, is a gentle giant beloved by millions of people around the world.

Written by respected author and world renowned underwater photographer, Doug Perrine, Ripley's *Whales and Dolphins* is full of fun facts and unbelievable tales culled from the Ripley archives and marine biologists around the world. *Whales and Dolphins* is the second in a series of six Ripley's Believe It or Not! books on Marine Life. We hope you enjoy reading *Whales and Dolphins* as much as we enjoyed researching and writing it.

Edward Meyer
Series Editor

top—Robert Ripley with his illustration for the story of "The Modern Jonah" (see page 49) as drawn for a movie short in 1931.

middle—Ripley fed the dolphins in a tank at St. Augustine, Florida's oceanarium during a live radio broadcast on February 23, 1940.

left—Ripley owned a 10-foot long narwhal tusk and proudly displayed it in his home. These tusks are often credited with the origin of the unicorn myth.

Introduction

Robert Ripley's
*Sunday color
cartoon
originally
published
April 22, 1945*

*L*ike many people, I was introduced to the wonder of marine mammals as a youngster by watching the Flipper television program. This show, among other things, helped to spark my early interest in marine biology as a career. Growing up in Northeast Ohio helped too, because a Sea World marine park was built nearby, and I spent a lot of time watching Bottlenose dolphins and Killer whales demonstrating their awesome behaviors in their daily performances.

However, it wasn't until I was college age that I really gained a true appreciation for the agility, intelligence and wonder of these magnificent creatures. It happened in the Gulf of Mexico aboard a scientific research vessel. We were steaming out of port when all of a sudden a huge pod of Bottlenose dolphins appeared all around us. There were hundreds of them "porpoising" as far as the eye could see. I scrambled up to the bow of the boat with others on board and looked straight down to watch these animals riding the bow wake of our vessel. We were very close to these animals and from above you could see them zigging and zagging back and forth, skillfully and rapidly changing positions, seemingly for fun! Their blowholes opened and closed quickly and sprayed water mist up at us, making a deep breath "woosh" noise as they breathed. They did this for only a few minutes and then disappeared as magically as they had appeared. Although I later discovered that dolphins riding a bow wake is a fairly common occurrence, this was up close and personal to me and cemented my interest and appreciation of these unbelievably graceful and intelligent animals.

More recently, I had a similar close encounter with large whales. I was lucky enough to go on a trip to San Ignacio Lagoon in Baja California in Mexico where the large California Gray whales are known to congregate. Although these animals prefer cold water where their food sources are, they migrate to warmer waters to give birth. San Ignacio Lagoon is a huge bay where hundreds of these animals come to breed and give birth. We went out one day in a large skiff with one of the very well regulated whale watching companies. After a very short boat ride, we were in the middle of the lagoon with large breaching whales all around us. After only a few minutes, a mother whale and her calf approached us and began to swim back and forth near our boat. The mother even lifted our boat out of the water a few times in the process of "scratching her back" on the boat hull. After "checking us out," she allowed her calf to get close to us. The calf seemed very curious about us and allowed us to pet, scratch and rub its body. Everyone on the boat was able to do this and everyone was completely thrilled by the experience. Although the calf kept coming back, after awhile the mother nudged her calf away and both disappeared. We had many such encounters that day and I will never forget the experience of coming so close to these beautiful giants.

If you're interested in marine mammals like I am, Ripley's Whales & Dolphins will answer all your questions and provide some of the latest scientific information about these intelligent, intriguing and enchanting animals.

Joseph M. Choromanski
Vice-President Husbandry
Ripley Aquariums, Inc.

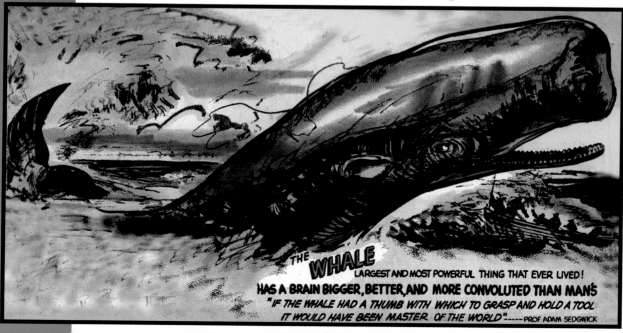

THE WHALE
LARGEST AND MOST POWERFUL THING THAT EVER LIVED!
HAS A BRAIN BIGGER, BETTER, AND MORE CONVOLUTED THAN MAN'S
"IF THE WHALE HAD A THUMB WITH WHICH TO GRASP AND HOLD A TOOL IT WOULD HAVE BEEN MASTER OF THE WORLD" ----- PROF. ADAM SEDGWICK

Contents

Introduction—Whales and Dolphins 2

Size Matters 6

Creatures from the Black Lagoon 10

What's the Difference? 14

The Whale Hall of Fame 25

Surviving the Sea 36

Nobody knows 42

Whales and People 48

Glossary 58

Index 59

WHALES *and Dolphins*

I f you go to Hawaii in the wintertime, and stick your head underwater, you might hear some very strange sounds. You might hear something that sounds like a bunch of chattering monkeys, followed by a sound like a chainsaw. You might hear squeaks, squeals, chirps, grunts, growls, moans, wails, whoops, and sounds that simply defy description. Some of the noises might sound as though they are produced by electronic equipment. Some residents of the Islands used to believe that they were coming from secret Navy submarine tests. The truth is even stranger.

These sounds are the calls of Humpback whales that come to Hawaii in the winter to breed. Humpbacks belong to a group of animals known as cetaceans, which includes whales, dolphins, and porpoises. When we say "whales" in this book we will be referring to all cetaceans, including dolphins and porpoises. Cetaceans are mammals, although they are very different in appearance from such familiar mammals as cows, horses, dogs, cats, and humans. The great writer Herman Melville, after carefully considering the matter in his classic novel *Moby Dick,* came to the conclusion that whales are fish, but he was wrong.

Whales have no vocal cords— yet they can be heard one mile away.

The fluke of a whale moves up and down to propel the animal, while fish move their tails from side to side.

Whale's milk contains 50% butterfat— 13 times as much as cow's milk.

Melville was fooled by the changes which occurred in the whales' bodies when they evolved from their land-dwelling ancestors to animals that, like fish, are completely at home in the sea. The need to move easily through seawater caused whales to evolve a fish-like body shape, and a fluke, which is similar to the tail of a fish, but is flattened from top to bottom, rather than from side to side.

Whales cannot extract oxygen from seawater like fish do with their gills. Like all mammals, they breathe air, give live birth to their young and then nurse their babies with milk that is rich in energy, vitamins, and protein. Very few fish care for their young in any way. Most fish just cast their eggs into the sea, and are done with them.

Whales, like this Humpback, give live birth to their young, and nurse their calves just like all other mammals do.

At first glance, whales do not appear to have hair, as do other mammals. However, if you look closely, you can see tiny whiskers on the "nose" and "chin" of this Southern Right whale.

Mammals are also distinguished from fish by the presence of body hair or fur. At first glance, it might not appear that whales and their relatives have any hair. However, if you look closely at the head of a Humpback whale, you can see a tiny hair sprouting from each of the bump-like tubercles on its head. Bottlenose dolphins do not have any hair during most of their lives, but before birth, the fetus has a few hairs on its snout. Some other cetaceans have a few bristles, which usually disappear before or soon after birth, but are reminders of their fur-bearing ancestors. The skin of most cetaceans is smooth, and they lack the scales that protect the skin of most fish.

Another difference between mammals and fish is that mammals are "warm-blooded," and fish are "cold-blooded." That doesn't mean that fish are always cold. Their bodies stay the same temperature as the water they swim in, but it does mean that mammals are always warm. They keep their bodies at the same temperature, regardless of how hot or cold it is around them. Of course, this amazing automatic control system only works while the animal is alive. When most mammals die, including humans, their bodies go cold. The body of a whale, however, is very well insulated. When a whale dies, its body can get so hot inside the blubber that the flesh actually cooks itself! Whalers sometimes found that their catch was ruined if they didn't butcher it promptly.

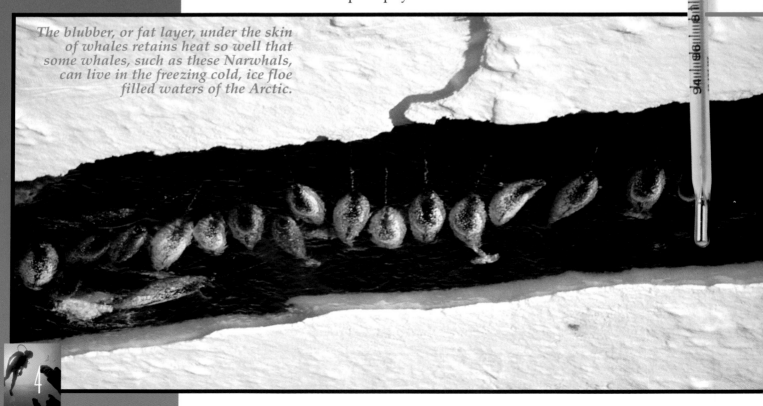

The blubber, or fat layer, under the skin of whales retains heat so well that some whales, such as these Narwhals, can live in the freezing cold, ice floe filled waters of the Arctic.

There are many other differences between fish and whales, but one that especially intrigues us is brain size. Fish tend to have small brains compared to mammals. Whales, dolphins, and porpoises, on the other hand, have brains that are among the largest of any animals, including humans, relative to their body size. In actual weight, the Sperm whale has the heaviest brain of any creature that has ever existed, weighing up to 20 pounds. Whale brains are also complex, with convoluted surfaces, like human brains. We still have very little understanding of how they use these huge, complex brains, but it is clear that cetaceans learn quickly, have good memories, and lead complex social lives.

Humans once killed so many whales that many species nearly became extinct. Some types are still in danger of disappearing forever. Recently humans seem to have fallen in love with whales and dolphins. Some people even worship them as gods, but some very basic facts of the lives of these attractive and intelligent creatures remain a mystery to us. It is ironic that we search the far corners of the universe for signs of alien intelligence, and yet invest little time and money in studying the intelligent life which is right here in our own oceans.

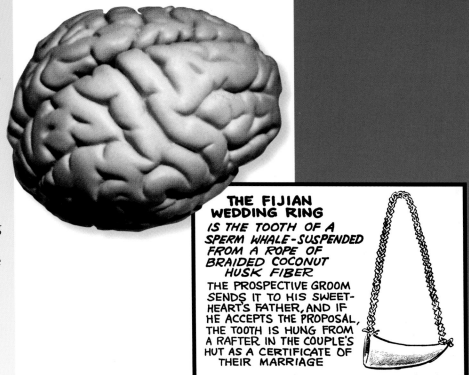

THE FIJIAN WEDDING RING IS THE TOOTH OF A SPERM WHALE – SUSPENDED FROM A ROPE OF BRAIDED COCONUT HUSK FIBER
THE PROSPECTIVE GROOM SENDS IT TO HIS SWEETHEART'S FATHER, AND IF HE ACCEPTS THE PROPOSAL, THE TOOTH IS HUNG FROM A RAFTER IN THE COUPLE'S HUT AS A CERTIFICATE OF THEIR MARRIAGE

Inuit, and other native peoples, have hunted whales for centuries. The traditional methods used by these cultures allowed them to kill only small numbers of whales to meet the needs of their communities.

It was once against the law in California to hunt whales from a car.

The efficient techniques of modern whaling and the practice of selling whale products resulted in whales being killed in great numbers. This Sperm whale was killed in the North Atlantic, near Holland, and lowered to shore for butchering.

Size Matters

Size MATTERS

Orcas can grow up to 30 feet long. Yet, scientifically, they are classified as dolphins! True whales can grow much larger.

It is not only the brains of whales that are large. Nearly everything about them is on a scale that boggles the imagination. Whales are the most awesome creatures ever to live on our planet. Even the largest dinosaurs were puny in comparison to the great whales.

The tongue alone of a Humpback whale can weigh two tons (4,000 lbs.), and its intestines can be nearly 200 feet long. This giant intestine is necessary to process the up to a ton and a half of food that the Humpback consumes each day during the summer-feeding season.

The teeth of Sperm whales normally grow up to ten inches long and two pounds in weight. This unusual specimen, however, measured 11 inches in length, and weighed four pounds.

Whales weighing 195 tons develop from the same size eggs as mice.

The tongue of this Orca is larger than its trainer's hand, but it is small compared to the tongues of the great whales upon which Orcas feed. Sometimes a pack of Orcas will kill a large whale just to eat the tongue, which can weigh two tons!

6

The adult Blue whale is the largest animal ever to live on Earth, reaching a maximum length of over 100 feet and a maximum weight of over 200 tons, as much as 24 full size African elephants! Some of its blood vessels are large enough for a child to crawl through. Its fluke is as broad as a soccer goal. Its spout is as tall as a three-story building. Its calf is born at a length of 23 feet, and a weight of nearly three tons! While nursing from its mother, the calf gains nearly 200 pounds a day. In seven months of nursing its calf, the mother may lose an amount of weight equal to the weight of a large dinosaur, and still weigh more than any dinosaur that ever lived!

"Big Hearted" A Blue whale's heart can measure six feet long and weigh up to 1,200 pounds!

The Blue whale is the largest animal ever to have lived, reaching a length of over 100 feet.

A Blue whale can equal the weight of 24 African elephants, or 32 average-sized Indian elephants.

Size Matters

A Blue whale mother and calf. The calves are born at a length of 23 feet and a weight of 3 tons.

The shrimp-like krill upon which Blue whales feed in California are only about ½ an inch long. In Antarctica, whales feed upon larger krill, measuring 2½ inches long.

Oddly enough, the largest whales, Blue and Fin whales, feed on some of the smallest creatures in the ocean—shrimp-like organisms called krill that are only ½" to 2½" long. Blue whales can eat over 8,000 pounds of krill in a day!

Whales did not develop such huge bodies due to over-eating, though. One of the main reasons they evolved large bodies was to retain heat. Heat loss is much more rapid in water than in air. When a ship sinks at sea, any passengers who do not make it into a lifeboat are likely to die of heat loss within a few hours. Larger people with more body fat will survive longer. This is one situation where being overweight has definite health advantages! As whales evolved larger bodies and thicker blubber, they were better able to retain body heat. This enabled them to exploit rich food resources in cold water. Larger body size also made it easier for them to migrate long distances to take advantage of these cold-water feeding areas. Being really big also means that you have fewer enemies that can attack you. For predators, like Orcas and Sperm whales, being big also means a bigger choice of things to eat. Orcas can eat anything from small herrings to Giant Blue whales. On land, gravity imposes limits on size, but in the ocean, gravity is counteracted by the buoyancy of water. Whales that are stranded on beaches may have their organs crushed by the weight of their own bodies.

During the spring and summer, Blue whales can eat up to four tons of food a day!

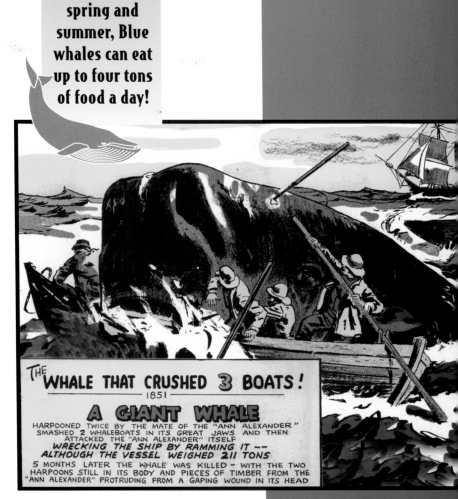

THE **WHALE THAT CRUSHED 3 BOATS!**
—— 1851 ——
A GIANT WHALE
HARPOONED TWICE BY THE MATE OF THE "ANN ALEXANDER" SMASHED 2 WHALEBOATS IN ITS GREAT JAWS AND THEN ATTACKED THE "ANN ALEXANDER" ITSELF
WRECKING THE SHIP BY RAMMING IT —— ALTHOUGH THE VESSEL WEIGHED 211 TONS
5 MONTHS LATER THE WHALE WAS KILLED – WITH THE TWO HARPOONS STILL IN ITS BODY AND PIECES OF TIMBER FROM THE "ANN ALEXANDER" PROTRUDING FROM A GAPING WOUND IN ITS HEAD

Inuit hunters peel the skin and blubber back from a whale, which they killed and dragged onto the icy shore.

9

CREATURES *from the* Black Lagoon

The prehistoric ancestors of today's whales lived on the land and hunted for fish along sea shores and in shallow lagoons.

The great whales evolved from much smaller ancestors. The earliest mammals, which appeared on earth over 200 million years ago, were tiny creatures no bigger than mice. Small size was probably an advantage in hiding from the ferocious dinosaurs that ruled the earth at that time. After the sudden mass extinction of the dinosaurs about 65 million years ago, mammals adapted into a variety of new forms to fill the ecological roles left vacant by the dinosaurs. Some grew larger than elephants.

The ancestors of whales and their kin were probably dog-sized animals that lived along the shores of a great shallow sea that separated India from Asia at that time. These were even-toed hoofed animals, related to the ancestors of sheep, cattle, antelope, and horses. The great reptiles, which had vanished from the earth, had dominated not only the land, but also the shallow waters of the earth. Their disappearance left a huge supply of fish in coastal seas and lagoons.

Fossil whalebones have been found in the center of America, hundreds of miles from the nearest salt water.

In 1990, scientists uncovered the bones of whales with hind feet that lived 40 million years ago in Egypt!

Although they may look like fish on the outside, the skeletons of whales show their relationship to other mammals. The arched jaws of this skeleton identify it as a Right whale.

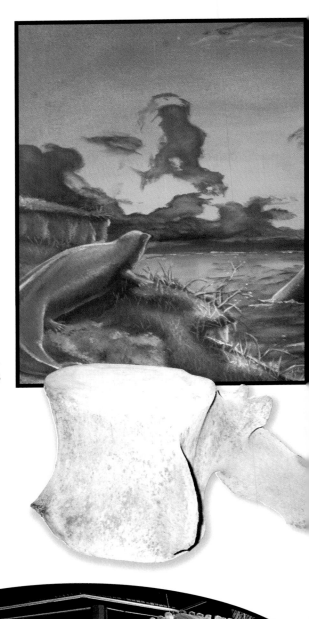

10

The pectoral fin of a whale is amazingly similar to a human arm with a "shoulder blade," an "upper arm," an "elbow," a "wrist" and 5 fingers.

It is likely that the early ancestors of cetaceans led a lifestyle very much like today's river otters—feeding in the rich waters of the warm lagoons bordering the coast, and returning to shore to rest and breed. Gradually they developed adaptations to enable them to dive and feed more successfully, and to spend longer periods of time in the water. The hind feet became webbed, then gradually smaller, and eventually disappeared as the tail enlarged, flattened into a fluke, and took over the main job of propulsion. Modern whales retain only a tiny hint of a pelvic bone where their hips used to be. The forelegs also became webbed, then flattened into flippers which were probably originally used for swimming, but now are used only for steering. Although whale flippers appear to be one solid piece on the outside, the internal bone structure looks very much like a human hand and arm, with "finger bones" corresponding to the toes of their land-based ancestors.

The nostrils gradually moved from the front of the snout to the top of the head, and developed watertight valves to seal them while diving. The external ears became smaller, then disappeared entirely, leaving only pinhole-sized openings. Sound is transmitted so much more effectively in water than in air, that a large sound gathering device was not needed. Big ears only created drag that slowed down swimming. Hearing actually became more important, though, as vision can be very restricted underwater, especially in the dark waters of coastal lagoons. The skulls of cetaceans began to change enabling them to process sound better. In some whales the lower jaw was modified to receive sound signals and carry them to the inner ear. Other organs developed to focus and transmit sound signals.

The "finger bones" of a whale's "hand" are derived from the toes of their land-dwelling ancestors. In life these bones are hidden inside a flipper that looks much like the fin of a fish.

Whales may have evolved from animals that lived very much like river otters.

Creatures

Fur was shed, leaving a smooth skin with minimal resistance to movement through the water. The job of retaining body heat was taken over by a layer of blubber under the skin. The blubber became thicker and thicker as whales evolved and increased in size. It also served as an energy storage area, enabling whales to go for long periods without feeding. This made long migrations possible. As the earth's climate and ocean circulation changed, the richest feeding areas moved from the tropics toward the poles. Whales could now swim to the polar regions to feed during the productive summer months, then return to the tropics to give birth in warm waters that would help the survival of their offspring. During these migrations they lived, like modern whales, only on the food-energy stored in their blubber.

Blubber also aids in buoyancy. Fat is lighter than water, and helps to counteract the weight of heavier parts of the body, such as bone, which cause an animal to sink. As whales adapted more fully to the aquatic environment, however, their bones became thinner, and less dense in relation to the increasing size of their bodies. Aquatic animals, which are supported partly by the water they live in, do not require skeletons as heavy as those of animals which live on land. In modern whales the skeleton makes up only about 15% of the body weight, versus 50% in land-dwelling mammals. Some whales have high oil content in their bones, which also aids in buoyancy. Some of the bones of Humpback whales are so light they actually float!

As whales evolved, their nostrils moved up to the top of their heads and became blowholes, which seal tightly when the whale is underwater, and exchange air rapidly and efficiently when it surfaces.

The whale and the kangaroo rat are the only mammals in all nature that have 6 of their 7 neck vertebrae fused together.

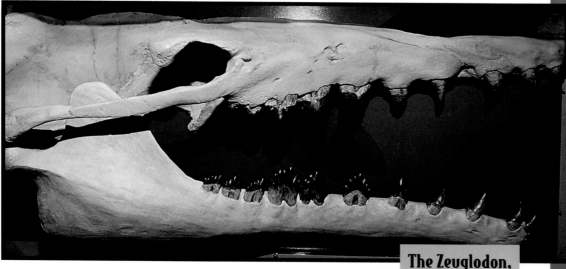

Forty million years ago, Egypt was covered with water, and was home to a prehistoric whale know as "Prozeuglodon." Note the huge sharp teeth for seizing and shearing its prey.

The Zeuglodon, a prehistoric ancestor of the whale, was 70 feet long, had a slim tapering body and propelled itself with a single pair of flippers.

As the mysticetes evolved, they lost their teeth. The job of capturing food was taken over by baleen, which looks like a fringe hanging from the upper jaw of this Gray whale.

The earliest fossils of web-footed amphibious mammals are about 50 million years old. These animals, like their shore-dwelling ancestors, lived by catching fish and other aquatic animals in their large teeth. Sometime in the next 15 million years, one group of early cetaceans learned to catch even smaller and more abundant marine organisms by gulping water and straining it out through their teeth. Gradually the teeth were replaced by new structures, called baleen plates, which took over the job of filtering food from the water. These plates, made of a substance similar to human fingernails, have frayed edges that join in fibrous mats that trap even very small food organisms. This group of whales began to specialize in feeding on small shrimp-like creatures and small schooling fish. These became the mysticetes, or baleen whales.

By 25 million years ago, another group of cetaceans had developed an improved method of finding larger food organisms. Rather than merely looking or listening for fish, these whales projected sounds into the water, and listened for the echoes to bounce off of their prey. This method of finding food, and navigating, proved so efficient that these whales were able to out-compete the other toothed whales, and gave rise to the modern toothed whales, or odontocetes.

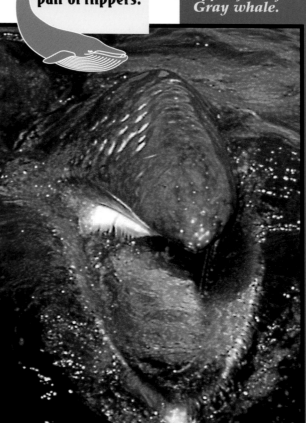

The earliest whales were toothed whales. They evolved both into baleen whales and such "super predators" as the Orca or Killer whale whose jaws are shown here.

Pilot whale
18 feet

Gray whale
45 feet

Sei whale
50 feet

Baird's Beaked whale
35 feet

Bowhead whale
50 feet

What's the Difference?

Between 25 million years ago and 7 million years ago, the two main groups of cetaceans—toothed whales (odontocetes) and baleen whales (mysticetes) diversified into a variety of species and adopted the

Killer whale
25 feet

Humpback whale
45 feet

Right whale
50 feet

Cuvier's
Beaked whale
20 feet

Bottlenose dolphin
9 feet

Blue whale
90 feet

Narwhal
14 feet

Minke whale
25 feet

Fin whale
75 feet

Bryde's whale
45 feet

...y Right whale
16 feet

Sperm whale
55 feet

basic shapes found in today's whales, dolphins, and porpoises. There are 70 known species of toothed whales, including dolphins and porpoises, and 12 species of baleen whales.

What's the Difference?

There are fundamental differences in the biology, social structure and behavioral patterns of toothed whales, such as these Atlantic Spotted dolphins, and baleen whales, such as this Humpback.

When humans first ventured out to sea, and encountered these creatures, the evolutionary relationships between the different species were not known, so people gave them common names based on obvious characteristics, such as size. The smallest cetaceans were called porpoises, larger ones were called dolphins and the really big ones were called whales. But different common names were applied in different places, leading to considerable confusion. Even more confusing is when the same common names are applied to unrelated creatures. Many fishermen, for example, use the word "porpoise" for all dolphins and porpoises, and use the word "dolphin" for a type of fish, also known by the Spanish name "dorado" and the Hawaiian name "mahimahi."

To a scientist, the word "porpoise" does not apply to just any small cetacean, but only to the six members of the family Phocoenidae, which all share similar characteristics that are believed to represent their evolutionary descent. Similarly, the word dolphin, as used by scientists, applies specifically to members of the family Delphinidae, and to the 3 families of river dolphins. In this system of naming, Pilot whales, Killer whales, and Melon-headed whales are all considered dolphins, because they all belong to the Delphinidae. Scientists believe that all the members of any one family are more closely related to each other than they are to any members of any other family.

For the past 150 years, Bottlenose dolphins have helped fishermen off the coast of Brazil catch mullet by chasing them into nets!

The Mysticetes
■ *Baleen Whales*

The order Cetacea is divided into two suborders: the mysticetes and odontocetes. Mysticetes (derived from the Greek words for "mustache whales") have a "mustache" of baleen hanging from the roofs of their mouths. Teeth are formed during development of the embryo, but are lost before birth. The baleen has the job of capturing all their food. Vast quantities of water are taken into the mouth, and then squeezed out through the baleen, trapping the food on the inside of the baleen. Baleen is also known as "whalebone," although it is not made of bone, but of a horny substance similar to hair or fingernails. In the days of whaling, baleen was used to make women's corsets, coach whips, umbrella ribs, shoe horns, fishing rods, and a variety of items for which plastic is now used.

Baleen whales also differ from toothed whales by having two blowholes rather than one. The shape and size of the spout produced when a whale exhales through its blowhole is distinctive for each species of whale. Baleen whales have a raised ridge called a splash guard in front of the blowholes which is absent in toothed whales. There are four families of baleen whales.

> **A baleen whale's mouth provides enough "whalebone" to make 10,000 brooms.**

Mysticetes, or baleen whales, have double blowholes, whereas odontocetes, or toothed whales, have a single nasal opening.

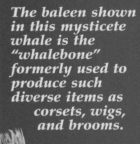

The baleen shown in this mysticete whale is the "whalebone" formerly used to produce such diverse items as corsets, wigs, and brooms.

The Difference

Baleen Whale Anatomy

Double blowhole

Baleen Plates

Dorsal fin

Pectoral fin

Fluke

Throat pleats

Pygmy Right whales (left) are classified in a separate family from the other Right whales, including the Bowhead whale (right), and the Southern Right whale (below).

The "bonnet" on top of a Right whale's head is one of several callosities which harbor large numbers of whale lice. Scientists are still debating why these odd patches of rough skin evolved.

The Right whale family includes Bowhead whales and Southern and Northern Right whales. Whalers considered them the "right" whales to hunt because they are slow moving, easy to harpoon, full of oil, and float after death. Right whales have the longest baleen of any whales. To make room for the long baleen plates, they have huge block-like heads, with bowed jaws. They feed by swimming slowly at the surface of the water with their mouths open, skimming microscopic shellfish called copepods from the water, and straining them out through their baleen. They do not have the expandable throat pleats found in lunge-feeding whales, and also lack dorsal fins. Northern and Southern Right whales, but not Bowhead whales, are marked by odd patches of rough skin on their heads, called callosities, which are infested with small crab-like whale lice that give them a white, or sometimes a yellowish or reddish color. Northern Right whales are the most endangered of all whales. Only about 300 survive in the North Atlantic, and even fewer in the North Pacific.

The Pygmy Right whale is classified in its own family. It is similar in appearance to the true Right whales, but has a small dorsal fin, and is much smaller in size. It grows to a length of only 20 feet and a weight of 3 – 4 tons, compared with lengths of nearly 65 feet and weights of over 60 tons reached by the true Right whales.

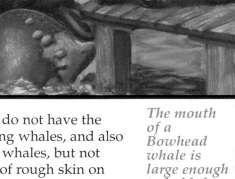

The mouth of a Bowhead whale is large enough to hold the contents of two large dump trucks.

18

There are seven species in the family of rorqual whales: Humpback whales; Fin whales; Sei whales; Bryde's whales; Blue whales; and Northern and Southern Minke whales.

All rorquals have a dorsal fin, a head that is flattened on top, and throat pleats (up to 90) which can expand like an accordion during feeding. These pleats allow enormous amounts of food and water to be taken in through the jaws that can open at nearly right angles. Rorquals rarely practice skim feeding—gulp feeding is their normal method of nourishment. They range in size from the 20 – 35 foot Minke to the 65 – 110 foot Blue whale.

The Humpback whale is in a genus by itself, and differs in appearance from the other rorquals, which are all grouped in the same genus. Humpbacks are not as sleek and smooth-skinned as the other rorquals, and have much longer pectoral fins.

The Gray whale is placed in a family by itself. Gray whales are of medium build, not as stocky as Right whales, but not as slender as rorquals. They only have a small hump instead of a dorsal fin. They have short, coarse baleen, which they use to filter organisms buried in ocean bottom sediments. There are one or two pairs of throat grooves, but no expandable pleats like the rorquals have. Their skin is usually mottled with patches of barnacles and whale lice. They grow to a length of nearly 50 feet and a weight of 30 tons. The population in the eastern Pacific has recovered from near extermination by whaling in the 1930s to over 20,000 individual whales now. The western Pacific population, however, is much smaller. The North Atlantic population of Gray whales was completely annihilated by the early 1700s.

To feed, a Humpback whale increases the size of its throat by temporarily dislocating its jaw.

The Difference

The "whale lice" infecting the skin of this baby Gray whale below the eye are crustaceans found at the drift line on beaches, and not insects like the lice that sometimes infect humans.

Minke whales are the smallest of the rorquals. Some scientists consider the Minke whales of the northern and southern hemispheres to belong to separate species, while others consider them to be a single species.

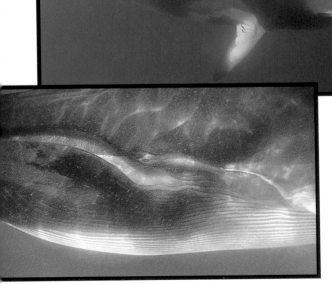

This Fin whale is feeding by straining water through the baleen which is visible through the open mouth. Fin whales are the second largest of the rorquals, after Blue whales.

THE LARGEST CREATURE EVER WEIGHED A **BLUE WHALE** 89 FEET LONG AND TOTALING **300,707 POUNDS** WAS WEIGHED AT SEA!

IT WAS DISMEMBERED AND WEIGHED PIECE BY PIECE ON 4 SCALES EACH CAPABLE OF HANDLING ONLY **200** POUNDS AT A TIME

Aboard the Hashidate Maru 1947

Spermaceti oil, which is actually more like wax than oil, can be solid or liquid, depending upon its temperature.

No one has ever seen a Sperm whale feeding, but we know that scenes like this occur because of the giant squids that have been found in the stomachs of Sperm whales. Most squid eaten by Sperm whales are smaller than the giant squid, which can grow to 70 feet—even longer than a Sperm whale.

The Odontocetes

■ *Toothed Whales*

The toothed whales are divided into nine families. All have a single blowhole, and hunt individual prey, rather than filtering large numbers of small animals from the water, as do baleen whales. All odontocetes have teeth, but in a few cases they are hidden inside the gums. There are a wide variety of body shapes among toothed whales. In general, they have more bulbous foreheads than baleen whales, in order to house the melon, an organ that is believed to be used to focus sound beams for echolocation (whale "sonar"). This organ is not developed in baleen whales, which are not known to echolocate, although it is possible they do.

Sperm whales are the largest of the toothed whales. They are so different from other whales that they are placed in their own family. They have the largest heads of any whales. In males, the head can be as much as one-third of the body length. These huge heads are filled with a fine oil, which made them valuable to whalers. The best oil is found in a long sac called the spermaceti organ. This oil is gooey and whitish in color. The earliest whalers mistook the oil for the whale's reproductive fluids, and named these whales Sperm whales because they had so much of it. Another odd thing about the heads of Sperm whales is that the blowhole is not in the center of the head, like on most other whales. It is offset to the left side, and points at a forward angle, instead of straight up, as on other whales.

Pygmy Sperm whales and Dwarf Sperm whales were formerly classified with Sperm whales, but are now placed in their own family. Like Sperm whales, they have a square shaped head, with the blowhole offset to the left, but they are much smaller. Pygmy Sperm whales can reach eleven feet in length while Dwarf Sperm whales grow to only nine feet. Both species have underslung jaws that give them a vaguely shark-like appearance, and odd markings on the side of the head that look just like the gill cover of a fish. Both have skin that is smooth (not wrinkled like a true Sperm whale), and a proper dorsal fin, instead of just a hump, like a true Sperm whale. The dorsal fin of the Dwarf Sperm whale is slightly larger than the dorsal fin of the Pygmy Sperm whale.

Toothed Whale Anatomy

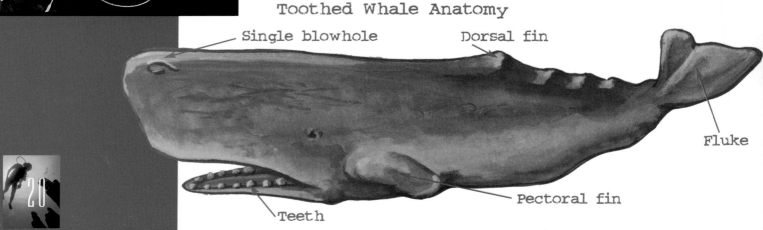

Single blowhole

Dorsal fin

Fluke

Pectoral fin

Teeth

The white whale family includes two species: Narwhals and Belugas. The females of the two species are somewhat similar in appearance, except that Narwhals have a "salt-and-pepper" splotchy coloration, while adult Belugas are either pure white or yellowish white. The calves are born dark, but lighten as they age). Belugas have 8 – 11 teeth in each jaw. All Narwhals have just two teeth, both in their upper jaw. In females both teeth stay hidden inside the jaw tissues, but in males the left tooth grows right out through the front of the head to form a tusk up to ten feet long. The tusk is used in ritual fighting during the mating season in somewhat the same way as antlers are used by deer and moose. Outside of mating season, males usually travel separately from females and juveniles.

The family of beaked whales includes 20 species and there may well be additional species that have not yet been discovered. Beaked whales live far offshore, dive deep, and spend little time at the surface. In general they avoid boats, and are rarely seen by humans. In fact, some species have never been seen alive! Everything we know about these rare species has been determined by studying dead bodies or skeletons. Beaked whales range in size from the 11-foot Pygmy Beaked whale to the 42-foot long Baird's Beaked whale. Beaked whales have small dorsal fins placed far back on their body, and have a smooth rear edge on the fluke without the notch which separates the two sides of the flukes of most whales and dolphins. They have beak-like snouts, with the lower jaw often extending slightly past the tip of the upper jaw, and only 1 – 2 pairs of teeth. They have a single pair of throat grooves.

Belugas are sometimes called the "canaries of the sea," because of the noises they make. During sound production, the melon often changes shape, and may bulge forward, as in the whale on the right.

This male Dense-beaked whale has scars that probably come from fighting with other males. The two bumps on top of the head are the tusks, which erupt only in males, and are always covered with barnacles.

The Difference

A huge white whale caught off Newfoundland in 1878 was shipped to London, England, wrapped in seaweed in a packing case. It completed the 5-week voyage in excellent condition.

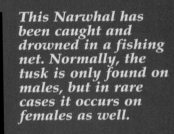

This Narwhal has been caught and drowned in a fishing net. Normally, the tusk is only found on males, but in rare cases it occurs on females as well.

Narwhal males cross tusks like fencing swords in ritual combat, but only rarely use them as actual weapons.

Beluga whales are attracted to classical music and can be led out of potential harm in icy waters by serenading them from the back of boats.

21

Hourglass Dolphin
5 feet

Rough-Toothed
Dolphin
8 feet

Indo-Pacific hump-backed Dolphin
6 feet

Finless Porpoise
5.5 feet

False Killer Whale
18 feet

Common
Dolphin
7 feet

Pacific Pilot Whale
20 feet

Dall's Porpoise
5 – 7 feet

Burmeist...
Porpois...
6 feet

Spotted Dolphin
7 feet

Spinner Dolphin
6 feet

Spectacled Porpoise
5 – 7 feet

Harbor Porpoise
5 – 6 feet

Irrawad...
Dolphi...
6 feet

Risso's Dolphin
13 feet

Bottlenose Dolphin
11 – 13 feet

Bouto
9 feet

Commerson's Dolphin
4 feet

Killer Whale
25 feet

Franciscana
6 feet

Northern Right
Whale Dolphin
7 feet

White Flag
Dolphin
8 feet

Tucuxi
4 feet

Ganges susu
9 feet

Hector's Dolphin
4 feet

Southern Right
Whale Dolphin
6 feet

Cone-shaped teeth are a feature of the family Delphinidae, or "oceanic dolphins." This dolphin is showing its teeth to the photographer in a threat display.

The Delphinidae

There are currently 33 recognized species in the oceanic dolphin family. These include most of the familiar dolphins, such as the Bottlenose dolphin seen on the popular television show *Flipper*.

Dolphins have 260 teeth— more than any other mammal.

These Striped dolphins are traveling at high speed by "porpoising" out of the water. While moving through air, they have less drag, enabling them to move more rapidly.

Pilot whales, sometimes called "Blackfish," are regular performers in marine parks and are excellent jumpers.

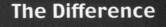

Also included in this family are the large dolphins sometimes called "Blackfish," or by their common names, Killer whale (Orca), False Killer whale, Pygmy Killer whale, Pilot whale, and Melon-headed whale. Members of this family range in size from 4 – 5 foot long Hector's dolphins to 15 – 30 foot Orcas, and also display a variety of body shapes and color patterns. Most, but not all, dolphins have a fairly long beak and have a large dorsal fin. The most distinguishing characteristic of the oceanic dolphins is their large cone-shaped teeth.

Indo-Pacific humpbacked dolphins can be white, gray, or pink. They may bear some resemblance to Pink river dolphins, and sometimes they do enter rivers, but they are members of the oceanic dolphin family.

The Pacific white-sided dolphin of the North Pacific is very similar in appearance to the Atlantic white-sided dolphin of the North Atlantic, but it is a separate species.

The Beiji, Baiji, or Yangtze River dolphin, may be the rarest dolphin in the world. It is in great danger of becoming extinct due to destruction of its habitat, and to accidental capture in fishing gear.

These Atlantic spotted dolphins look very much like Pan-tropical spotted dolphins, but by studying differences in the skulls and genetic analysis scientists have placed them in different species.

Nobody is really sure how Risso's dolphins, or Gray grampus, come by the scars that usually cover the bodies of adults, but it is most likely a result of fighting among themselves.

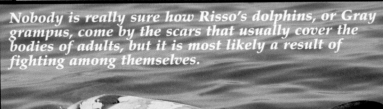

23

The Phocoenidae

Ganges River dolphins are completely blind and use ultrasonic signals to find their way.

The six members of the porpoise family, by contrast, have sharp-edged spade-shaped teeth. All porpoises are small, ranging in size from the 4 – 5 foot long Vaquita to the 6 – 8 foot long Dall's porpoise. All porpoises have blunt snouts with no beak. Most, but not all, have a dorsal fin, which tends to be triangular, rather than curved like the dorsal fin of the Delphinidae.

■ *River Dolphins*

River dolphins are actually more closely related to porpoises than they are to the oceanic dolphins. The five species of river dolphins are classified in three separate families. Their similar looks are not due to shared ancestry, but to the fact that they have all adapted to similar environments. The three families are distinguished primarily by differences in their skulls and teeth. All river dolphins have long narrow snouts with many narrow teeth suited for catching fish and other small prey. Since the rivers they live in are often dark and murky, they have come to rely primarily on their sense of hearing, and their eyes have become very small. Some can barely see at all.

Harbor porpoises are rarely photographed because they do not approach boats or swimmers, as dolphins often do. They are most likely to meet humans only as a result of becoming trapped in fish nets, fish traps, and trawls.

A Beiji, or Yangtze River dolphin catches a fish in a tank at a research facility in China. Breeding of captive dolphins such as this one may be the only thing that saves the Beiji from extinction.

Vaquitas often get entangled in fish nets. As a result, they have become the most endangered of all the porpoises. Only a small number survive in the northern part of the Sea of Cortez.

THE HALL OF FAME

In this chapter we will take a closer look at some of our favorite cetaceans—Sperm, Humpback, Blue, Gray, and Right whales, Orcas, Bottlenose dolphins, Dall's porpoises, and Amazon River dolphins.

Sperm Whales

Sperm whales are the largest toothed whales. Males grow to over 60 feet in length, and females to just over 40 feet. Immortalized in the novel *Moby Dick*, the block-headed shape of the bull Sperm whale has become a general symbol for whales. But no other whale looks anything like this—not even the female Sperm whale. Only large males have the huge square head seen in cartoon drawings of whales. All Sperm whales have prune-like wrinkled skin completely different from the smooth hydrodynamic skin of other cetaceans. With only a low hump for a dorsal fin, and very small pectoral fins that normally lie flat against the body, Sperm whales look more like big wrinkled logs than like their sleek dolphin cousins.

The behavior and social structure of Sperm whales is also very different from that of other cetaceans. In fact, the social organization of Sperm whales is more similar to that of elephants than to other whales and dolphins. Females travel in stable pods with their juvenile offspring of both sexes. They roam around a bit, but generally stay within certain areas in the tropics and subtropics. They take turns "baby-sitting" each others' infants, which stay at the surface while the adults are diving deep for food. Males leave the pod when they reach adolescence, and begin to travel in bachelor pods. As they mature, they become solitary, and roam all the way to the poles, feeding in the rich, cold waters of the Arctic and Antarctic. Only the largest males are able to breed. When they return to the warm waters closer to the equator, they rove from one pod of females to another, looking for opportunities to mate. When two males fight over access to females, they may seriously injure each other with their large teeth.

These ivory teeth seem to be mainly used in fighting and they do not even protrude from the gums until years after the whales begin feeding. Sperm whales feed mostly on soft-bodied squid, which can be swallowed whole, without the need of teeth. While on feeding dives, Sperm whales make regular clicks that sound like carpenters at work, or horses' hooves on pavement. It is generally believed that these clicks are used to echolocate food. However, squid do not reflect sound as well as fish. Some scientists have suggested that perhaps Sperm whales make loud clicks to stimulate light-producing plankton, and use that light to see the squid in the darkness of the depths where they feed. However they find them, Sperm whales do catch a prodigious amount of squid of all sizes. The giant squid, which may grow up to 70 feet long, resist being swallowed, as attested by dinner-plate-sized scars on the heads of some Sperm whales (left by suckers armed with hooks on the squid's tentacles), but are still no match for a hungry Sperm whale.

top- A Sperm whale arches its back at the surface as it begins a dive, showing its unusual wrinkled skin.

middle- The broad tail flukes are the last part to disappear beneath the surface when a Sperm whale dives.

bottom- Sperm whales are the largest toothed whales. Males grow to over 60 feet in length and females to just over 40 feet.

Hall of Fame

In 1988, Henry, a 35-foot-long Humpback whale, swam into New York City harbor and traveled all the way up the Hudson River to 86th Street.

One of the most distinguishing features of the Humpback whale is its long oar-like pectoral fins, which look like wings when extended.

Humpback whales breach frequently, displaying their unique markings and coloration.

Humpback Whales

Of the Humpback whale, Herman Melville wrote, "He is the most game-some and light-hearted of all the whales, making more gay foam and white water generally than any other of them." These acrobatic habits have made Humpbacks a favorite of whale-watchers. Humpbacks breach more than any other great whale—sometimes dozens of times in succession. They also often slap the water with their great pectoral fins and thrash it with their flukes. Their pectoral fins, or flippers, are the longest of any whale—up to 17 feet long. That's nearly a third of their body length, which can be up to 50 feet in males. Females grow somewhat larger, and may exceed 60 feet in rare cases. Their long fins give Humpbacks more maneuverability than other whales.

Humpbacks do not appear as sleek and streamlined as other members of the rorqual family. Besides their big, lumpy pectoral fins, their bodies are fairly chunky, and their heads are covered with bumps called tubercles that make them look like big black pickles. About the only thing that could make them look more odd and ungainly would be if they were actually hump-backed, but despite their name, they are not physically deformed. They may have originally been given their name because of the way they arch their backs before diving. As the animal rolls forward to complete the dive, the fluke is often lifted high in the air, revealing a pattern on the underside that can range from pure white to pure black or a mixture of both. This pattern is unique to each individual, and is used by researchers to identify particular whales.

In spite of their odd appearance, Humpbacks move through the water with marvelous grace and precision. Like most wild animals, they tend to avoid humans and their machines, but some bolder individuals exhibit curiosity toward people, and even approach boats seeking interaction. Although all cetaceans use sound for communication, Humpbacks are the only whales that actually sing. All of these characteristics have endeared them to humans perhaps more than any other whales.

Humpbacks, like all baleen whales, feed by straining water through their fibrous baleen. Their maneuverability and clever feeding techniques, however, allow them to capture not only tiny shrimp-like creatures, but also a variety of small schooling fish, up to the size of mackerel. In the summer they remain in cold waters gorging themselves day and night on schools of herring and shoals of krill. As they feed, they add to their blubber layer, increasing it up to as much as six inches in thickness. The blubber serves both to keep them warm, and as a source of energy when they are not feeding.

In the winter, a few Humpbacks remain in the feeding areas, but most migrate to the tropics—a voyage of up to 5,000 miles each way—where breeding occurs. Very little food is available to the whales on their trip, and in the breeding areas, so most do not eat at all for several months. It may be that they leave their feeding grounds because they have to burn too much fat just to keep warm in the cold winter water, or it may be that the main reason for the grand excursion is that the babies are born with only a thin layer of blubber and would not survive well in very cold water.

Whatever their reasons for making this incredible journey, the whales pay for it by consuming their own blubber layer, becoming noticeably thinner and losing a great deal of weight as the winter progresses. You might imagine that they would try to conserve energy by resting all the time. Humpbacks do spend time resting in winter, but they also continue to perform active displays, including flinging themselves out of the water. Groups of males also chase females around while battling violently with each other. Whales wander around the breeding areas, and even make excursions out into open-ocean, sometimes traveling hundreds of miles on these side trips. Imagine the energy it takes to launch an 80,000 pound animal out of the water. Then imagine doing that a hundred times, swimming hundreds of miles, possibly getting involved in several brawls involving minor injuries and loss of blood, mating, breaching some more, and swimming thousands of miles back home, all without eating for over two months. Then imagine also giving birth and producing up to 50 gallons of milk a day to nurse the baby, all without a bite to eat!

Humpback whales in one ocean all sing the same "songs"— and change their tune each year.

Humpback whales have a small hump just in front of the dorsal fin, but some people believe their name comes from the way that they arch their backs when starting a dive.

When Orcas attack larger whales, they usually grab the flukes first. This Humpback's flukes are covered with white scars from the teeth of Orcas. (Photo taken under authority of NMFS research permit #882).

27

Gray Whales

Gray whales, like Humpbacks and male Sperm whales, are great migrants. Every year they swim thousands of miles between their feeding areas in the cold North Pacific and their breeding areas near the tropics and back again. Gray whales, however, do not occur south of the equator, and have been extinct in the Atlantic Ocean for at least 200 years, probably because their feeding areas, breeding areas, and migration routes were all close to shore where they could be easily disturbed and exploited by humans. Gray whales nearly became extinct in the Pacific, as well. After protection from whaling, the population on the eastern side of the Pacific recovered dramatically, but the population in the western Pacific did not. There are now more than 20,000 Gray whales which annually migrate from feeding areas near Alaska and Russia down the west coast of North America to lagoons in Mexico's Baja Peninsula where they breed.

Whale watching has become a popular activity along much of the migration route, but in the breeding lagoon at San Ignacio, Mexico, a phenomenon occurs that is unique in the world. Here whales regularly come over to play with the whale watching boats, sometimes lifting them out of the water on their backs. Whales "spyhop" next to the boats, and seem to actually beg to be petted. Mothers will even bring their newborn calves over to the boats and allow them to be stroked by humans in the boats.

The face that sometimes lifts out of the water to regard the whale-watchers from only a few feet away could be described as "grotesquely beautiful." Gray whales don't have the "stovebolt" knobs that adorn the heads of Humpbacks, but they do have a "complexion problem." Their faces and bodies are heavily infested with barnacles and small crab-like parasites, called "whale lice."

Their skin is a mottled gray. There is only a small hump on the back, instead of a dorsal fin, and behind this there is a series of bumps, or "knuckles." Their baleen is short, compared to the rorquals, and is mostly used to filter shellfish from mud that they suck off the bottom. Instead of the throat pleats that rorquals have, Gray whales have only two to five creases in their throats. They reach a length of just over 50 feet for females, and a little shorter for males.

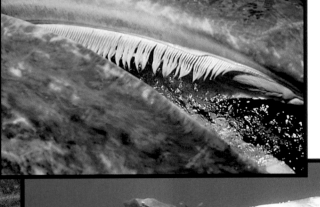

A juvenile Gray whale off California passes through a forest of kelp. The white spots on the whale's body are barnacles—crustaceans which build shell homes on the bodies of larger animals, and on the hulls of ships.

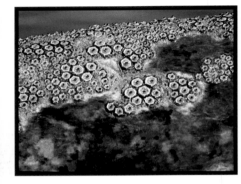

This Gray whale's skin is covered with barnacles. The area around the barnacles is infested with whale lice—small parasitic crustaceans that give a pink color to the barnacle patch.

Right Whales

Like Gray whales and Humpbacks, Right whales make breeding migrations to bays and other shallow areas that offer protection for the newborn calves. Unlike Grays and Humpbacks though, Right whales feed in the open ocean, often far from shore. They swim slowly at the surface, with their mouth open in a wide "grin," letting water flow in the front and out the sides, through the baleen, trapping food against the inside of the baleen as it flows out. In two hours, a Right whale can filter a million gallons of water, and collect over a billion tiny copepods, collectively weighing more than a ton. They also feed on other plankton, but not on fish.

Since they feed without gulping or sucking, Right whales do not need any throat pleats, like those of the rorquals, or throat creases, such as Gray whales have. Like Gray whales, they are heavily infested with whale lice, but these are mostly confined to the odd growths called "callosities" which decorate their heads. The largest callosity, called the "bonnet," is on top of the head. The placement, shape, and size of the callosities are different for each individual, enabling researchers to tell them apart. Females can grow to a length of 60 feet; males slightly less.

Whereas in other types of whales the males often compete violently for access to the females, male Right whales are more likely to cooperate to move a female into position for mating, and may take turns with her. The real competition is not to mate, but to father her calf. Each male produces enormous amounts of semen in order to improve his chances of being the one that impregnates the female. Part of the strategy for success is to flush out as much of the other whale's semen as possible. Scientists call this type of mating strategy "sperm competition." To be successful, male Right whales have developed the largest testes in the animal kingdom, weighing up to 1,000 pounds each.

There are two species of Right whale, the Northern and the Southern. They are very similar in appearance, but there are slight differences in the skull and in the callosity patterns. Southern Right whales are recovering from over-exploitation during the whaling days, and the population is increasing steadily. Northern Right whales, however, are the most critically endangered whales in the world. Some scientists believe that they are doomed to extinction in spite of our efforts to protect the few that remain.

Hall of Fame

A Southern right whale and a diver eye each other with mutual curiosity. Whales rarely exhibit aggression towards humans unless attacked, but still can be dangerous because of their size and power. Even a playful baby whale can cause serious injuries, so experts do not recommend swimming with whales.

Right whales are the only whales known to hold their flukes high out of the water for long periods. No one is certain why they do this, but it may help them to adjust their body temperature, or it may merely be a form of play.

The pattern of callosities on Right whales varies, but there are always callosities over the eyes.

29

The Blue whale, which has a mouth so large a full-grown man could stand in it with his hands raised, can swallow nothing larger than a shrimp.

Swimming Blue whales are sleek and graceful in appearance. They are so long that it is almost impossible to photograph the entire body of a Blue whale underwater. Usually a diver can only see part of a Blue whale's body at a time.

The tail of a Blue whale is the broadest of any animal. The flukes can stretch 25 feet from tip to tip.

Blue Whales

Blue whales were also believed to be headed for extinction by the time they received international protection. Most populations remain small and imperiled, but at least one off the coast of California, appears to be recovering. Blue whales are similar in appearance to other rorquals, especially Fin whales, Sei whales, and Bryde's whales, but can be recognized by the mottled pattern on their blue-gray skin. Especially in cold water, the underside may become coated with tiny plants called diatoms that give the whale a yellowish color. For this reason they are sometimes called "sulfur bottom whales." Blue whales grow much larger than any other whale—larger than anything else that has ever lived. While most people think of them as being huge fat blobs, they are actually quite slender, but very long—growing up to 100 feet for males, and 110 feet for females.

Blue whales are high-speed swimmers. They specialize in feeding on krill, which are shrimp-like animals that are both larger and more mobile than the copepods on which the much slower Right whales feed. Krill occur in very dense swarms. Blue whales race from one patch of krill to another, swallowing an entire school before the krill have a chance to get out of the way. The Blue whale's head is broad and U-shaped on top. Underneath, the throat is pleated from the chin all the way to mid-belly. The 55 to 68 pleats allow the throat to balloon out to enormous size as the mouth opens, so that the krill and all the water surrounding them can be taken in at once. The water is then squeezed out through the baleen plates, leaving the krill trapped inside. Especially when the pleats are expanded, a Blue whale resembles the world's largest tadpole, with a bulging head that just looks way too big for the slender body tapering out behind it.

Most Blue whales migrate between cool waters where food is more abundant, and warmer waters where breeding occurs, but some populations appear to stay in the same general area year-round. Blue whales sometimes gather together when feeding, but generally do not travel in groups or form large breeding aggregations. Blue whales may be able to keep track of each other from hundreds of miles away. Their calls are both extremely loud, and of very low frequencies (too low in most cases for our ears to hear). Low frequency sounds travel very well in salt water. Scientists have recorded the sounds of a Blue whale that was over 1500 miles away!

Some scientists believe that Blue whales make these moans to "keep in touch," find mates, and so forth. Others believe that the sounds are a type of long-range sonar, enabling the whales to "map" the ocean floor and know their position at all times, even in the middle of the open ocean. Neither idea has been proven, but it is certain that these whales have remarkable abilities that we are just beginning to understand. Crossing an ocean for a Blue whale may be like walking across the neighborhood for us.

When feeding, the appearance of a Blue whale changes dramatically. It gulps in water and krill until its throat bulges out like a giant balloon stretching from its lower jaw to its belly button.

30

Orcas—Killer Whales

Blue whales may be the largest, loudest, and most powerful creatures on earth, but they are no match for the biggest member of the dolphin family, the Orca or Killer whale. Although they reach a length of only a little over 30 feet for males, and a little under for females, Orcas are able to prey upon even the greatest animal in the sea. They are able to capture Blue whales and other great whales by a combination of speed, agility, cunning, and teamwork. The ability of Orcas to hunt together successfully, and defeat prey that they would be unable to capture alone, is a result of the tight bonds between members of their family pod. Orcas stay with their mothers for their entire lives, so all members of a pod are directly related. Although their attacks on their prey can be savage, Orcas are tender and affectionate with their pod members. Some packs of Orcas roam the oceans attacking whales, dolphins, sea lions, sharks (including fierce Great Whites), rays, turtles, penguins, and almost anything else large enough to satisfy their appetites. Other pods "stay at home" within a relatively confined area, subsisting on a steady diet of fish. Some researchers believe the differences between these two types of Orcas are so great that they should be considered separate species.

Breaching almost entirely out of the water, an Orca displays the distinctive "tuxedo" color pattern of black and white that makes it easy to distinguish Killer whales from other large cetaceans.

This breaching Orca can be identified as a female.

Dolphins have no sense of taste or smell.

The conical teeth in the mouth of this Orca identify it as a member of the family Delphinidae, or oceanic dolphins. The teeth are designed for seizing and holding, not cutting. Cetaceans swallow their food whole.

The two varieties of Orcas can be easily distinguished by their unique calls, but their appearance is essentially identical. Orcas cannot be confused with any other cetaceans, however. They are instantly recognizable by their "tuxedo" color pattern with a black back, white belly, and white eye patches. A light gray "saddle patch" just behind the dorsal fin is variable in form and shading and allows recognition of specific individuals by researchers. The dorsal fins of males grow much taller than those of females, and can reach a height of nearly six feet! The large, rounded, paddle-like pectoral fins of Orcas are distinctive from the more sickle-shaped flippers of other dolphins.

While Orcas prefer cool water where prey is abundant, they roam throughout the world's oceans, from the poles to the equator. There are permanent resident pods off the coast of Washington State and British Columbia, and perhaps elsewhere, but most Orcas appear to be nomadic, traveling long distances in search of food. Some show up predictably at certain locations where food is seasonally abundant. One example is in the fjords of Norway where Orcas appear every fall to feast on the great schools of herring that are present at that time. The Orcas circle the herring and drive them into a compact ball, then smack them with their tails to stun them before feeding. Orcas show up off the coast of Argentina every year when the sea lions have their pups. To seize a pup, the Orcas will actually launch themselves up onto the beach, then wriggle back into the water with the baby sea lion between their jaws.

Stories of such behavior caused a great deal of human fear of Orcas before they gained immense popularity as performers in marine parks and films. At times they may show interest and curiosity, but Orcas do not eat humans and usually avoid people when possible.

An Orca stalks a juvenile sea lion on a beach in southern Argentina.

The Orca has stranded itself on the beach in order to seize the baby sea lion. When the next wave comes in i will wriggle back into the water wit its catch. This unusual hunting method is learned from older membe of the Orca pod.

Bottlenose Dolphins

As with Orcas, individual Bottlenose dolphins may differ greatly in their lifestyles, with some living as permanent residents in near-shore areas, while others travel widely. Likewise, some experts believe there may actually be at least two different species of Bottlenose dolphins. Different populations may also differ in appearance, especially in size. Offshore populations, and those found in colder water tend to be larger and stockier than those found inshore and in warmer water. Bottlenose dolphins off of Europe can surpass 13 feet in length, while those in the warm coastal waters of Florida seldom reach nine feet.

Bottlenose dolphins get their name from their relatively short, stubby beak, with a pronounced crease where it joins the head. They are mostly gray, but are usually lighter on the sides than the back, and lighter still on the belly. Sometimes the belly is spotted, and it may turn pink from blood flow during heavy exertion, such as jumping.

Because Bottlenose dolphins are often found close inshore, and because they thrive in captivity, and are easily trained, they are the most familiar to us of all the dolphin species. Television shows and movies have led many people to view all dolphins as *Flipper*. Researchers who work with dolphins, however, know that Bottlenose dolphins can be violent and mischievous.

The "Flipper" characterization, however, is unfair. As with any widespread, intelligent, and highly social animal (such as ourselves), Bottlenose dolphins exhibit a wide variety of behavior patterns—some that meet our approval, and some that don't. Bottlenose dolphins occur throughout the world's oceans, except near the Polar Regions, but only a few populations have been well studied. The best known is a group of dolphins that live off the West Coast of Florida. In this population, most adult females belong to groups consisting of females and their calves. Youngsters form subadult groups when they are old enough to leave their mothers. When the females have their first calf, they usually re-join the mother's group. When males mature, however, they form partnerships with one or two other males, or live alone.

Bottlenose dolphins feed mostly on fish, which they catch by a variety of ingenious methods, including whacking them up into the air with their tails; driving them up onto river banks and snatching them off the mud; working as a group to herd them together and taking turns eating them; and using echolocation to find them and dig them out of the ocean bottom sand. They also eat other animals, such as octopus and squid. In Portugal, researchers found that octopus had devised a way to defeat Bottlenose dolphins that were preying on them, by climbing on the dolphin's head and covering its blowhole to prevent it from breathing!

DOLPHINS ONLY SLEEP 2 HOURS AT A TIME AND ALWAYS KEEP ONE EYE OPEN!

Bottlenose dolphins are coastal cetaceans which can enter shallow water, and are sometimes found around coral reefs. Bottlenose dolphins have even been seen scratching their backs on soft corals.

Dolphins send out sonar signals through their foreheads and receive them back through their jaws.

Bottlenose dolphins are generally considered playful and friendly, but some dolphins have been known to attack and kill porpoises for no apparent reason.

Dall's Porpoise

Porpoises have as many as 96 teeth—yet they swallow their food whole.

The markings on Dall's porpoises are somewhat similar to those of Orcas, but they are much smaller than Orcas. In fact, Orcas often prey upon Dall's porpoises.

Porpoises and some whales prefer cold waters, but they can freeze to death if trapped in icy waters. In 1884 a large whale was discovered near the South Shetland Islands completely entombed in an iceberg over 300 feet high.

Dall's porpoises are unusual among the family of porpoises for several reasons. For one, they grow larger than most porpoises, up to 8 feet long and nearly 500 pounds for males, and up to 7 feet long for females. They are found only in the North Pacific, in waters colder than 55 degrees Fahrenheit, from California north to Alaska, and from Japan north to Siberia. Their rotund, stocky bodies are well adapted to the cold waters in which they live.

While most porpoises are shy, avoid boats, and have "calm dispositions," Dall's porpoises swim at high speed, and often rush over to boats to ride the bow wave. They move along the surface so fast that they usually kick up a "rooster tail" as they swim.

Their color pattern is also distinctive, and much more flamboyant than the dull gray of most other porpoises. Their bodies are black on top, with a white patch on the belly that extends up onto the sides, somewhat like the pattern of an Orca, but without the eye patches. There is often a white or light gray edging on the dorsal fin and/or the fluke.

Each year, thousands of Dall's porpoises are accidentally killed in fishing nets. Many others are deliberately captured for food.

Dall's porpoises can dive deep, as well as swim fast, giving them access to a wide variety of food sources. They eat fish such as herring that school near the surface, fish that live in mid-water in deep-ocean, and fish that live on the bottom. They also eat crabs, squid, and other animals. They are sometimes preyed upon by sharks, but their main enemy is the Orca. Orcas are sometimes seen pursuing Dall's porpoises at high speed, with both animals kicking up rooster tails. When the Orca catches up, it may toss the porpoise high into the air before consuming it. A much greater threat to Dall's porpoises, as well as most other porpoises, however, is gill nets, in which thousands die every year. In Japan, and some other countries, they are also deliberately killed for food. Very little research has been done on the Dall's porpoise, and little is known about their social structure, habits, and natural history.

Amazon River Dolphins

The pink river dolphin is also known as the Amazon River dolphin, Boto or Boutu. It lives in South America's Amazon and Orinoco Rivers and their tributaries. Individuals range from pink to white to gray or blue-gray. There is a long hump along the back in place of a dorsal fin. The beak is very long and narrow, with cone-shaped teeth in front for catching fish, and flat molars in back for crushing armored fish or shellfish. The eyes are tiny, but can apparently see well, in contrast to other river dolphins that are nearly blind. Nevertheless, echolocation is probably much more important than vision for capturing food in the murky waters of the Amazon basin. Like Belugas, pink river dolphins can change the shape of their melons while producing sounds. The neck is very flexible for a dolphin, allowing the head to be turned at right angles to the body while "scanning with sonar." Additionally, the beak is lined with hairs that are believed to be sensory organs, like the whiskers of a cat. They may be used to feel for food or obstacles at close range.

Botos are usually seen alone, or in pairs, but sometimes occur in-groups of up to twenty. They swim slowly, compared to other dolphins, and usually make only short dives, of less than two minutes. Their lives follow the rise and fall of the river, and the flooding of the rain forest. Like other river dolphins, they are threatened by destruction of the forest around the river, development along the river itself, and fishing. Some of the new settlers moving into the Amazon hunt and kill the dolphins, but, in general, they are not eaten. Many of the jungle tribes have legends, superstitions, and taboos concerning river dolphins.

An all-white fresh-water dolphin was found in 1918 in Lake Tung-Ting, China, but it is the only one of its kind ever seen.

Some Amazon River dolphins are pink, but others occur in various shades of gray. All have a long tubular snout and small eyes.

Amazon River dolphins are able to hunt fish in very shallow water using echolocation. During the rainy season they can actually swim into the rain forest to hunt.

Surviving

SURVIVING
IN THE SEA

lthough baleen and toothed whales have taken very different evolutionary paths, they have both adapted superbly to the demands of the ocean—resulting in bodies that are very different from those of their closest land-dwelling relatives. Whales, dolphins, and porpoises can move through the water in an extremely efficient way, with a minimum of drag. The fastest dolphins and porpoises are able to swim unaided for short periods at speeds close to thirty miles an hour.

Scientist suspect that the reason cetaceans are able to achieve such high speeds is partly due to their soft, spongy skin, which may be able to absorb turbulence created as the animal moves through the water. Naturally, engineers who design ship hulls are very interested in trying to copy this effect, but so far they have had only limited success. Most cetaceans have beautifully streamlined bodies. Organs which hang outside the bodies of land mammals are tucked into slits in the bodies of whales and dolphins. Oil glands in the skin of cetaceans may also aid them in locomotion by actually greasing their passage through the water.

When dolphins and porpoises really want to move quickly, they do so by leaving the water entirely. In a motion called "porpoising," they leap repeatedly from the water. While moving through the air, they escape the drag of the water, and can attain greater speeds over a long distance. They do this both while fleeing danger and while pursuing food.

At other times, when resting or searching for food, whales may stay underwater for long periods. Most cetaceans can stay submerged for at least 20 minutes, while some deep-divers, such as Sperm whales and Beaked whales, can stay down for an hour or more.

8 MEN RODE THE BACK OF A WHALE!
THEIR 22-FOOT WHALEBOAT WAS CARRIED THROUGH THE BERING SEA 6 FEET ABOVE THE WATER

Many types of whales are seldom seen by man and new species are still occasionally sighted, and named. The animal in this picture, taken by a sea captain in the 1930s, has never been identified. Capt. George Peck estimated this "Blackfish" to be nearly 50 feet long. The animal is shown swimming alongside a ship traveling in the ship's wake.

Pygmy killer whales prey upon other marine mammals, as well as upon fish and squid. The white scars on their sides probably come from fighting with each other.

Divers have to carefully limit their time and depth to avoid "getting bent" as a result of absorbing too much nitrogen from the air they breathe. Cetaceans avoid this problem by allowing their lungs to collapse when they dive, preventing nitrogen from being absorbed from the lungs into the bloodstream.

I t is easy to imagine that in order to stay down so long, whales must have enormous lungs. This, however, is not the case. Their lungs are not any larger in relation to the size of their bodies than are the lungs of land mammals. They, however, work more efficiently. Cetaceans exchange 80 – 90% of the air in their lungs with each breath. The air may be expelled at up to 300 mph after surfacing from a dive. In humans only about 15 – 20% of the air is exchanged while at rest, and 70 – 80% is exchanged during heavy exercise. You might be even more surprised to learn that whales do not hold any air in their lungs when they dive. Instead, the lungs collapse, and the remaining air is forced into the windpipe.

This is how whales are believed to escape the deadly condition called "the bends" which affects scuba divers who go down too deep, for too long. Air is composed of nitrogen and oxygen. Both gases are forced from the lungs into the bloodstream under high pressure. The oxygen is used by the body, but the nitrogen merely dissolves in the tissues. When a diver ascends, and the pressure is reduced, the nitrogen can bubble out of the tissues, just as bubbles form in a bottle of soda that has been uncapped. These bubbles can block blood flow to vital organs, resulting in "the bends." By not carrying air down in their lungs, whales avoid this complication.

Whales are also able to extend their diving times by slowing their heart rate, and by shifting blood flow to only the most vital organs, such as the brain and heart. Champion breath-hold divers often study yoga to help them mimic the diving reflex that comes naturally to cetaceans.

The Grampus can swallow a seal whole and then disgorge the skin—which is mysteriously removed in the stomach of the Grampus.

A whale clears its lungs with a loud "whoosh" when it comes to the surface. The visible "blow" or "spout" can reach 30 feet high.

etaceans have very keen senses that are different from those of land mammals. The greatest differences appear to be in the sensing of odors, which carry more easily in air, and sounds, which carry better in water.

Baleen whales still retain small organs of smell, and it is possible that they use these to detect odors released into the air by concentrated swarms of plankton or fish, but it appears that the toothed whales may have lost the sense of smell altogether.

Taste is a very useful sense in the water. It is likely that many whales use taste not only to locate and evaluate food, but also to obtain information about other members of their species in the area. Chemicals secreted into the water or released in waste products could enable other animals to recognize the individual that released them, conveying information about sexual condition, social status, and other important characteristics of the animal. It is speculated that cetaceans may also use taste for navigation, as salmon do when searching for the rivers from which they entered the ocean as juveniles.

Some River dolphins can probably only detect differences between light and dark, but most cetaceans have excellent vision. Many can see well in both air and water, and some are known to regularly lift their heads out of the water to look around, a behavior called "skyhopping." Some species have good color perception, but others, which live mostly in deep blue ocean waters, may detect only blue light well. With their eyes set wide on either side of their heads, most cetaceans can see nearly all the way around them—a useful feature in the ocean, where danger can come from any direction. There is also an area of overlap, where both eyes can focus on an object at the same time, to give distance perspective.

More important even than vision to cetaceans is the sense of hearing. While vision is limited to an effective range of just over 100 feet in water, sound can transmit information over hundreds of miles. Scientists are beginning to suspect that some whales can communicate with each other across entire ocean basins. The low frequency moans made by baleen whales may also function as a crude kind of sonar. Such sounds can travel great distances, and may reflect off of undersea mountains and other features, enabling whales to know exactly where they are in the ocean, despite being able to see only open blue water all around them.

The large eye is an indication that most dolphins have good eyesight, but the more important sense organ is probably the snout. It is believed that the lower jaw receives the echoes from sound signals that are broadcast through the melon in the forehead, and passes them to the ear.

> **In 1991, three dolphins, following a school of fish, swam up Italy's Tiber River and spent 6 hours in the heart of Rome!**

Many cetaceans can focus their eyes in air as well as in water. Some like these Melon-headed whales, spyhop often, getting a look at what's around them above the water.

38

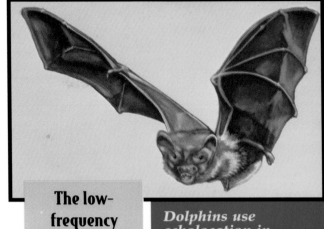

oothed whales produce higher frequency sounds, which are useful at shorter distances as high definition sonar. This ability is effective for finding food and avoiding predators and obstacles at close range. A series of clicks are typically used for this purpose. They may sound something like dragging a comb across a microphone, or even like a squeaky door. Bats use the same technique to catch insects in the dark.

Listening to the echoes of a rapid series of clicks can give a dolphin so much information about an object that it can probably form an acoustic "picture" of that object. Because the sound waves can penetrate soft tissues, like flesh, the acoustic image gives a picture of internal structures and organs. In this way, dolphins may be able to "look" inside other dolphins to "view" their health and emotional state. Dolphin sonar can also penetrate bottom sediments to a depth of several inches, enabling dolphins to easily locate and capture fish hiding under the sand. Treasure hunters have attempted to train dolphins to locate gold and silver buried under bottom sand, and though dolphins are able to recognize precious metals, most treasure is buried much deeper than their sonar can penetrate.

Other sounds are used to communicate with other members of the same species. Dolphins often communicate with high-pitched whistles. Some whistles are used to identify the individual making the call—as if the dolphin was calling "I'm Maria, I'm over here!" Whistles and other sounds can also express emotions. We do not yet know if any whales use true language, where sounds are arranged in variable patterns to express abstract concepts, but experiments have shown that dolphins do have the ability to use a simple language if it is taught to them.

The low-frequency sounds made by Blue whales measure up to 188 decibels—louder than a jet plane—and can be detected up to 500 miles away!

Dolphins use echolocation in much the same way as bats. By emitting ultrasonic calls and listening for the echo, dolphins can catch fish and navigate cavern passageways in total darkness.

Atlantic spotted dolphins are sometimes seen to cruise slowly near the bottom, or even to stop and lie on the bottom propped on their fins, as if listening for something. Sounds travel best close to the bottom, so they may well be obtaining information about something that is too far away to be seen.

Surviving

A Sperm whale dives towards the abyss. In the ocean depths, where there is little light, these whales may depend upon senses other than vision to find food.

A dolphin can distinguish between a sheet of aluminum and one of copper—even if both are painted the same color.

Orcas travel in pods that are formed of tightly bonded family groups. Each pod has a distinctive dialect, and researchers can recognize the pods by their calls alone.

Some dolphins can hear sounds with frequencies ten times higher than what we can hear, and others can hear sounds three times lower than humans can hear. Dolphins can even hear sounds one and a half octaves higher than what a dog can hear. Large whales are hard to study, so it is difficult to know the range of their hearing, but they must be able to hear the low-frequency sounds they themselves produce. Whales can probably also detect the sounds made by swimming schools of fish or even krill. Whales can also tell what direction a sound is coming from underwater—something that we are unable to do.

Some whales may have an additional sense for navigation—one that is totally unfamiliar to us. A form of iron called magnetite has been found in the heads of some cetaceans. This may enable them to detect the Earth's magnetic field, as if they had a built-in compass. It may also enable them to read the magnetic patterns in rocks on the sea floor as if they were reading a map.

The more familiar sense of touch is well-developed in cetaceans. Their entire body surface seems to be extra sensitive to even the slightest pressure, and can respond to the water disturbance around an object without even having physical contact with the object. Touch is often used to reinforce social bonds. Social groups may spend hours rubbing against each other.

Long-term social bonds generally seem more highly developed in toothed whales than in baleen whales. This is not surprising, since many toothed whales must hunt cooperatively to survive, while baleen whales are more likely to be successful "grazing" as individuals. The most tightly knit cetacean society is that of Orcas. Orcas tend to stay with their mothers for life. A pod may consist of three or more generations of mothers, grandmothers, and their offspring. To avoid inbreeding, mating occurs when two pods come together. In some other species, such as Sperm whales and Bottlenose dolphins, males leave the pod when they reach adolescence, wandering in small groups of males, or becoming solitary.

Humpback whale lunge-feeding in Alaska. One variation of this feeding method is bubble-netting, which requires close coordination between the individual whales to capture fish trapped within a curtain of bubbles released by the whales.

Even a dolphin's acute senses cannot protect it from injury by motorboats moving at high speed. Every year whales and dolphins are injured and killed by collisions with boats. This is a major threat to the recovery of highly endangered Northern right whales.

In baleen whales, by contrast, calves typically leave their mothers as soon as they are weaned. There is little evidence of long-term social bonds among baleen whales. One exception is the stable feeding groups of Humpback whales, which have been observed year after year in Alaska. These whales actually hunt schools of herring cooperatively. One or more individuals may blow curtains of bubbles that frighten the fish into a compact ball. Then the entire pod of whales lunges through the school of fish with their mouths open. Most remarkable is that each individual whale seems to come up in the same position relative to the others on each feeding lunge.

Juvenile toothed whales often play together, learning social roles and developing bonds that will be important in adulthood. Young dolphins may travel in "nursery schools" with adults taking turns watching them. Baleen whale calves have much less contact with other youngsters. Humpback mothers actually keep other calves away from their offspring.

Dolphins are very social animals capable of showing several emotions. When a dolphin dies, other dolphins in its pod actually gather around the dead body and hold a vigil that may last for several hours.

We are only beginning to learn about the social lives of whales and dolphins, and recent research has turned up many surprises. For example, while many people think of dolphins as always being gentle and loving, they can also be mischievous and violent. Male Bottlenose dolphins have recently been discovered to engage in activities that, if they were performed by humans, would be very aggressive.

We are also learning that the behavior and social structures of different species are very different from each other. Each species must adapt to the requirements of its own unique place in the environment. The more we learn about these remarkable and intelligent creatures, the more we are surprised by what we find out!

The calf of a Blue whale is 23 feet long at birth, consumes half a ton of milk a day for 6 months and gains 220 pounds each day

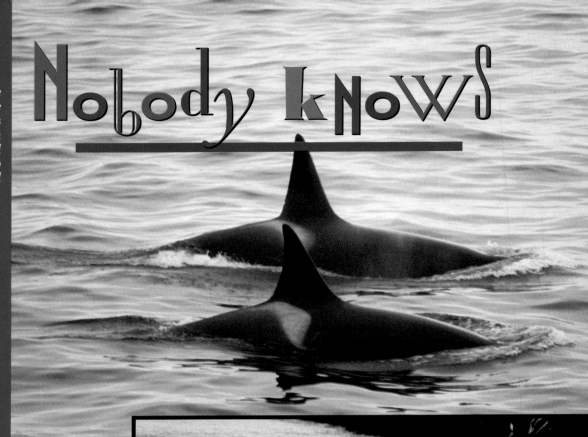

Nobody Knows

The light saddle patches behind the dorsal fins of Orcas vary between individuals, and allow researchers to recognize individual Orcas for studies.

A snow-white whale 54 feet long and weighing 55 tons was caught by the whaler Anglo-Norse in the Pacific Ocean on August 12, 1951.

This Minke whale which stranded on the beach and died, will be dissected by scientists, but such studies often fail to tell us how the animal died, much less how it lived.

Until quite recently, most of what we knew about cetaceans came from dissecting carcasses of animals that had died or been killed. In recent years, however, more and more scientists have taken to studying live whales and dolphins in their natural habitat. Our knowledge of the lives of these amazing creatures has increased dramatically in the last 30 years. What we don't understand about them, however, is still much greater than the amount of information that we have learned. They remain creatures of mystery, and some aspects of their biology and behavior are absolutely baffling!

Researcher Mark Ferrari uses a hydrophone to listen for the songs of Humpback whales on the winter breeding grounds in Hawaii. The whales in Hawaii sing the same songs as Humpbacks in Mexico and Japan, even though the songs are constantly changing. (Photo taken under authority of NMFS research permit).

Mysteries of Migration

Humpback and Gray whales undertake the longest migrations of any mammals. Every year they swim back and forth from their feeding grounds near the poles to their breeding grounds near the equator, a distance that can be over 10,000 miles—round trip. Incredibly, they feed very little or not at all during this entire three month long trip, including the time they spend on the breeding grounds. For many years, nobody knew what migration route Humpback whales used to get from their feeding grounds in Alaska to their breeding grounds in Hawaii. The migration path of Gray whales on the other hand can be followed all the way down the West Coast of North America, and quite a few whale-watching businesses are based on this predictable movement. Humpbacks, however, just seem to vanish from one place and mysteriously appear in another.

By attaching tags with satellite transmitters to whales, scientists were finally able to track Humpbacks from Hawaii straight north across the open Pacific to Alaska. Not all of the tracks went north, however. One track went almost due east, and one went almost straight west! Where were these whales going? North Pacific Humpbacks do not breed only in Hawaii, but also in Japan and Mexico. Could these whales be visiting more than one breeding location in the same year? This would involve swimming thousands more miles, in addition to the 5,000-mile round trip between Alaska and Hawaii, without anything to eat the whole time!

Each year Gray whales swim down the west coast of North America to Mexico from as far away as Siberia. How they navigate is uncertain, but it may involve an internal magnetic compass.

Whale satellite transmitter

Whale-watchers also migrate to Mexico every winter, to meet the Gray whales on their breeding grounds. At San Ignacio Lagoon, friendly Gray whales, such as this calf, often approach the whale-watching boats, and allow people to touch them.

Whales traveling in line (such as these Humpbacks) may have given rise to sea serpent stories.

Humpback whales typically adopt a head-down posture, at a slight angle, and lie motionless while singing.

Humpback whales are the singing stars of the ocean. Scientists are not sure why the males sing, but because it occurs most frequently on the breeding grounds, it is surmised that it is to attract females, or establish territorial rights.

Vocal Mysteries

If Humpback whales do make these long trips to separate breeding areas during the same breeding season, it would help answer the really perplexing question about the Humpback's song. Humpbacks in Japan, Hawaii, and Mexico all sing the same song. The song, however, does not remain the same, but changes slowly throughout the breeding season. The changes miraculously occur at the same time in all the different breeding areas. Humpback singing is very loud, and can be heard for miles underwater, but certainly not across the thousands of miles of open ocean separating the three main breeding areas in the North Pacific. How can whales on one side of the ocean know what whales on the other side are singing, and copy it? To date, whales have not been shown to move between the different breeding areas in one season, but if they are found to do this, it will answer one of the mysteries of the Humpback's strange music.

Another unanswered question is why do Humpbacks sing? The songs of Humpback whales are the longest and most complex in the animal world. The facts that only males sing, and that most of the singing is done in the breeding areas, provide clues that singing is somehow connected with mating. Your first guess might be that males sing to attract females. Recent studies have shown, however, that rarely does a singer actually attract a female. In fact, it is usually another male that approaches! Scientists guess that the singing may play a role in establishing dominance, or in spacing out males on the breeding ground, but really no one knows for sure. We do not even know exactly how Humpbacks make these amazing sounds because they have no vocal cords!

RADIO STATION *ORCA-FM* in Vancouver, B.C., Canada 24 HOURS A DAY, PLAYED *NOTHING BUT THE SOUNDS of WHALES!* (1997)

DOOBIE DOOBIE DOO...

HUMPBACK WHALES CATCH FOOD BY SWIMMING IN A CIRCLE THEN BLOWING A HUGE TUBE OF TINY BUBBLES AROUND THEIR PREY!

Feeding Mysteries

We may not know how Humpbacks sing, but we do know how they feed. Some of their feeding techniques, such as bubble netting, almost defy belief, despite scientists having watched and studied this behavior for many years. On the other hand, nobody has ever seen a Sperm whale catch its food. From looking in the stomachs of dead whales we know that Sperm whales eat a variety of fish, but favor various kinds of squid, including the kraken or giant squid.

Humpback whales coordinate their moves when lunge-feeding in order to trap the maximum number of small fish. When they are not feeding they are not as social as toothed whales, but they will cooperate when it increases their feeding efficiency.

But how does the Sperm whale catch and subdue its slippery prey? You might guess that their enormous ivory teeth are used to seize the squid. These teeth, however, often do not appear until years after they have begun to feed for themselves. Even more baffling are the cases of caught whales that had broken or deformed jaws. In one case, the lower jaw was bent out at a right angle from the upper jaw, yet this whale had a full stomach! It has been proposed that the white lining of the mouths and lower jaws of Sperm whales reflect light created by plankton (tiny floating animals), which attracts the squid right into the whales' mouths. They may feed primarily by suction, as do Beaked whales. Another idea is the "Big Bang" theory, which suggests that the loud clicks made by Sperm whales while they are hunting can actually stun or kill their prey. The truth is, nobody knows for sure.

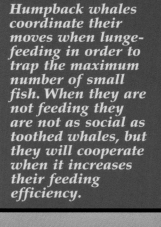

Whale's teeth were once legal currency on the Fijian Islands.

The soft bodies of squid do not reflect sound as well as animals that have bones and air spaces. Scientists debate whether Sperm whales can stun or kill squid by making loud noises, and whether they find them by echolocation.

45

Sperm whale's off-center blowhole

"Thar She Blows!"

Another mystery is the placement of the Sperm whale's blowhole. It is not directly on top of the head, as it is in other cetaceans, but at a 45-degree angle off to the left side. It looks like it would be hard to keep water out of it in this position, and observations confirm that this is the case. When Sperm whales in rough water surface to breathe, they sometimes have to bob their heads high out of the water to get a breath. The design cannot be dismissed as some type of accident of evolution, however, because both Pygmy Sperm whales and Dwarf Sperm whales also have blowholes that are offset to the left. This odd placement must offer some advantage that outweighs the obvious disadvantage that it is harder to keep it clear of the water. Yet nobody has ever come up with a convincing explanation of what that advantage might be.

A Finback whale weighing 70 tons was preserved with 8,000 quarts of formaldehyde and displayed in New York City and Europe.

Beautiful Symmetry?

Most animals have symmetrical bodies. That is to say, they look the same on one side as the other. Sperm whales, with their blowholes over on the left sides of their heads, are a notable exception. They are not the only cetaceans, however, whose left sides do not match their right. Fin whales are colored white on the right side of their head but gray on the left side. Orcas and Humpback whales appear to use the white coloration on the undersides of their bodies to flash light at the small fish they feed on and frighten them into a better position for feeding. Perhaps Fin whales circle their prey in a certain direction in order to use this technique. It has also been suggested that they use the white side of their face to signal other members of their species. Nobody really knows for sure how they use their color pattern, or even if they really use it for anything.

Fin whales are among the few animals with a face that is colored differently on the left side (above) from the right (below).

Mysterious Mimicry

In addition to puzzles relating to color, some whales have mysterious markings. For instance, the Pygmy Sperm whale and the Dwarf Sperm whale both have markings on the sides of their heads that look like the gill covers of fish. How would a whale benefit by disguising itself as a fish?

Large sharks and Orcas that might attack small whales also eat fish, so it is doubtful that the disguise would help protect the whales from predators. Everything these whales eat is also eaten by fish, so it would not appear that the disguise would help them sneak up on their prey. As humans, we have never had the experience of living in the open ocean, so it is difficult to conceive the value of this mimicry. If it did not enhance the survival or reproduction of these whales in some way, however, it would not have evolved.

The light marking on the cheek of the Pygmy Sperm whale looks just like the edge of a fish's gill plate cover.

The Most Baffling Mystery of All

One aspect of whale behavior that has baffled scientists for many years is their tendency to beach themselves on shorelines in groups to die. In some cases, whales that stranded in this way were found to have parasites or diseases that could have affected their ability to find their way, but in many cases, most or all of the whales were found to be perfectly healthy. Curiously, this self-destructive behavior occurs almost exclusively with toothed whales. It may be because these whales have tighter social bonds than do baleen whales. Perhaps only one whale becomes sick, or makes a navigational error, and the others refuse to leave it. Sometimes it appears that the geography of the shoreline, or even the magnetic patterns of the rocks underneath, may cause whales to become confused and swim into the beach. Pollution, predators, weather, undersea volcanic eruptions, explosive detonations, following prey inshore, and other factors have also been suggested as possible factors, but most strandings remain unexplained. Often stranded whales that are towed back out to sea merely swim a few miles down the coast and beach again. The sight of such beautiful animals destroying themselves is both sad and puzzling.

Strandings of baleen whales, such as this Bryde's whale in New Zealand, are rare. Most strandings are of toothed whales.

Toothed whales, like these Sperm whales in Oregon, because of their social nature, sometimes strand in large numbers. Scientists suspect that only one sick or disoriented whale may sometimes lead dozens to strand and die.

Thousands of years before Orcas were trained to act "cute" for theme park performances, they commanded the respect of tribal peoples, who recorded their encounters in art and legends.

The Makah tribe of North America was one of the earliest whaling nations on Earth. This stone carving located in Washington State, shows Orcas and human faces. The Makah have recently revived their ancient whaling traditions.

Whales & PEOPLE

Eskimo tombstone on the Island of Ka-y-ne, in the Bering Strait, are made of whale ribs.

S ince the earliest times, people have lived in awe, wonder, and often fear of the powerful forces of the natural world, and the mighty and mysterious creatures that dwell in it. Before the advent of scientific observation, explanations of the origins and nature of animal species depended primarily on the creativity of the storyteller. As the largest, most powerful, and most mysterious of the animals that early peoples contacted, whales naturally became the subjects of art and legends. Some of these legends have been passed down to modern times, and help to define the cultures that created them. While some cultures saw cetaceans as dangerous sea monsters, others treated them as friends of man, or even as gods. In recent years, as people have had more contact with whales and dolphins, attitudes have changed. Cultural differences in attitudes towards whales continue to cause conflict between different countries, and between different groups within countries.

The earliest known depiction of a whale is a sketch of an Orca, carved into a rock in Norway about 9,000 years ago. Artistic representations of cetaceans also appeared in ancient China, Greece, and Rome, and among the Native American tribes of the Pacific Northwest. All of these cultures, and many others, had mythological tales concerning dolphins and whales. The Greek god Apollo was said to have turned himself into a dolphin, and to have been worshipped at a dolphin shrine. In another Greek legend, sailors turned into the first dolphins after they jumped into the sea to escape the wrath of the god Dionysus. The Greek god of the sea, Poseidon, had his chariot pulled by a team of dolphins. Another Greek myth tells of Heracles who was swallowed by a whale, and lived in its belly for three days.

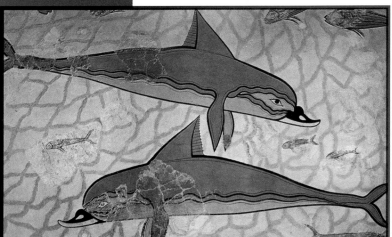

Stylized depictions of dolphins on a Minoan palace thousands of years old reflect the reverence in which early Mediterranean civilizations held these playful creatures, which were believed to bring good luck.

The myth of the unicorn may have been created as a "marketing tool" for Narwhal tusks. These tusks sold for fabulous prices in medieval times, and were credited with many magical properties.

The Modern Jonah

☐ Did a whale swallow the Biblical Jonah? Scientists declare that, although the whale is the largest animal that ever lived, its throat is so small that it will choke on a herring.

However, it is also conjectured that the Sperm whale may have been the "great fish" mentioned in the Bible. When mortally wounded the Sperm whale has been known to disgorge chunks of squid six feet long by four feet wide, and an 18-foot skeleton of a shark was found in the stomach of one, on another occasion.

Then, too, there is the account of James Bartley, an English sailor, who was actually swallowed by a whale, and later rescued.

This is a word for word translation of the French scientist M. de Parville from the Journal de Debats, 1914.

In February, 1891, the whaling ship Star of the East was in the vicinity of the Falkland Islands when the lookout sighted a large Sperm whale 3 miles away. Two boats were launched and in a short time one of the harpooners was enabled to spear the whale. The second boat attacked the whale but was upset by a lash of its tail, and the men were thrown into the sea, one man being drowned, and another, James Bartley, having disappeared, could not be found. The whale was killed in a few hours, its great body lying on the ship's side, while the crew busied itself with axes and spades removing the blubber. They worked all-

day and part of the night. The next morning they attached some tackle to the stomach of the whale and hoisted it on deck. Suddenly the sailors were startled by something in it that gave spasmodic signs of life. Inside was found the missing sailor doubled up and unconscious. He was placed on deck and treated to a bath of sea water which soon revived him but his mind was not clear and he was placed in the captain's quarters where he remained for two weeks a raving lunatic. He was kindly and carefully treated by the captain and the ship's officers and gradually regained possession of his senses. At the end of the third week he entirely recovered from the shock and resumed his duties.

During his sojourn in the whale's stomach, Bartley's skin where it was exposed to the action of the gastric juices, underwent a striking change. His face, neck and hands were bleached to a deadly whiteness, taking on the appearance of parchment [paper].

Bartley remembered the lash of the whale's tail and "then was encompassed by great darkness and he felt that he was slipping along a smooth passage that seemed to move and carry him forward. His hands came in contact with a yielding, slimy substance, which seemed, to shrink from his touch. He could easily breath but the heat was terrible. It seemed to open the pores of his skin and draw out his vitality. The next he remembered he was in the captain's cabin. While he recovered fully from his mental depression his skin retained its ghastly pallor to the end and never recovered its natural appearance.

The legend of Heracles is very similar to the story of Jonah, which appears in the Old Testament of the Bible. As originally written in Hebrew, the animal, which swallowed Jonah is described only as a "great fish," but when translated in the Gospel of St. Matthew, it becomes a "whale." Scholars are still debating whether the story is fact, fiction, or symbolism, and whether Jonah was actually swallowed by a whale, a whale shark (a type of shark as large as a whale), or a giant sea bass.

The Jewish holy book, the Talmud, tells of sailors landing on the back of a sleeping whale, believing it to be an island, and building a campfire, only to have the whale awaken and dive down from under them. The same legend reappears in Christian mythology of the Middle Ages, with the Irish monk St. Brendan as the sailor in one version.

The myth of the unicorn was created when traders brought Narwhal tusks to medieval Europe. Being unfamiliar with the whales that produced these amazing items, Europeans supposed them to have come from one-horned white horses. Legends of people turning into dolphins, and vice-versa, are common in many cultures. In the Amazon basin, villagers tell of Pink river dolphins, which turn themselves into men and come to dances to seduce the local women. It is said that you can recognize the dolphin-men because they always wear hats to cover their blowholes.

Many Native American tribes had elaborate mythologies explaining the origins of nearly everything they encountered in the natural world. On the Pacific coast these legends were often symbolically represented on totem poles that identified the lineage of the owner. Orcas were a popular symbolic totem figure.

A ncient Greek writings include not only myths about cetaceans, but scientific and historical accounts concerning them. The first cetologist, or whale scientist, was Aristotle (384-322 BC), who described various species of cetaceans, and correctly recognized them as mammals, more than 2,000 years before this became generally accepted. Some of the Greek and Roman accounts of dolphins describe behavior which we recognize as accurate today, even though they were widely disbelieved for hundreds of years.

In the epic historical poem, *The Odyssey*, Telemachus, the son of Odysseus (Ulysses to the Romans) was said to have fallen into the water and been rescued by dolphins. Many such stories are still told today. There are also numerous recent stories of dolphins protecting divers and shipwreck victims from sharks. There are now quite a few documented observations of whales and dolphins supporting a sick or dead individual at the surface or intervening to defend another individual from attack by sharks or Orcas. It is not difficult to believe that this helpful behavior could be directed towards humans as well.

Both Aristotle and the Roman historian Pliny the Elder wrote of lone dolphins which lived by the coast and befriended young boys, allowing themselves to be touched, giving them rides, and even grieving after the boys' deaths. This seems like fantasy, but similar relationships have been repeated numerous times in recent history in various countries. These dolphins are sometimes known as "ambassador dolphins." For some reason they no longer belong to a pod of dolphins, but choose to interact with humans instead. Some of the more famous "ambassadors" include "Pelorus Jack" and "Opo," both of New Zealand, JoJo of the Turks and Caicos, and "Hatteras Jack" of North Carolina. In the Bahamas, an entire pod of wild dolphins have become very friendly with people, and regularly approach boats to play with swimmers. While such dolphins seem to enjoy contact with humans, they can also get very upset when humans misbehave. A number of people have been injured by "friendly" dolphins when they tried to grab or ride the dolphin, or touched it near the eyes, ears, or blowhole. One man was killed in Brazil when he was rammed by an ambassador dolphin after trying to force an ice cream stick down its blowhole.

THE AMAZING PILOT PORPOISE OF HATTERAS INLET

"HATTERAS JACK" a white porpoise FOR A PERIOD OF 20 YEARS GUIDED EVERY SHIP IN AND OUT OF HATTERAS INLET, OFF THE COAST OF NORTH CAROLINA -- AND *NEVER LOST A SINGLE VESSEL!* IT WOULD SWIM AROUND EACH SHIP TO GAUGE ITS SIZE AND DRAW, WAIT UNTIL THE TIDE HAD REACHED THE PROPER LEVEL, THEN LEAD THE VESSEL SAFELY PAST THE TREACHEROUS SHOALS AND REEFS - "HATTERAS JACK" FIRST APPEARED IN 1790 AND DISAPPEARED IN 1810 WHEN THE PLACING OF BUOYS AND BELLS MADE HIS ASSISTANCE UNNECESSARY

For 36 years, a 14-foot dolphin named "Pelorus Jack" met and accompanied vessels through New Zealand's 6 mile long Cook's Strait. Pelorus Jack disappeared during World War I.

This modern Inuit engraving depicts an ancient legend in which a hunter who has harpooned a whale must decide whether to release the whale or risk drowning as it drags him under the icy depths.

Accounts of dolphins befriending children and giving them rides have appeared from the time of the ancient Greeks to the present. This painting depicts a 1991 news story from Bangladesh about a dolphin that rescued a baby swept out to sea by a tidal wave and carried the boy back to shore.

A WHALE OF A FUNERAL

Whales were once considered so sacred by Indo-Chinese fishermen that when a dead whale was found it was carried in a solemn burial procession on the same hearses used for royalty, and then was interred in the royal burial grounds. The fisherman who found the dead whale was considered its adopted son—and automatically assumed the title of Prince.

Fences around many homes in Ameland, The Netherlands, are made of the ribs and lower jawbones of whales.

A ristotle also related accounts of fishermen who were aided in their work by dolphins that drove the fish into their nets. Such a partnership seems incredible, but it occurs on a regular basis to this day between dolphins and fishermen in Mauritania, and in southern Brazil. There are also many stories of fishermen training River dolphins to herd fish for them on command. Perhaps it is partly for this reason that River dolphins are considered sacred in most countries where they occur. The Greeks considered it bad luck to harm any dolphin—an act that could invoke the wrath of the gods. In some parts of Vietnam all whales are worshipped, and sacred whale bones are kept in special temples.

In other cultures, such as Japan, and among the Makah Indians of Washington State, whales were revered, but were still killed. It was believed that the whale would voluntarily allow itself to be killed if the proper respect was shown, and the proper rituals completed.

It is not known when whaling actually began, but it was probably preceded by the discovery that many uses could be made of whales that died and washed ashore.

Their blubber could be used for fuel and medicine, the meat could be eaten, and useful and decorative objects could be created from bones, baleen, and sinews. The teeth of Sperm whales were used as money in parts of Polynesia, even though there is no evidence that the islanders ever hunted Sperm whales.

Scrimshaw—the art of engraving on ivory—is an age-old art form originally practiced by sailors on the teeth of Sperm whales. This example shows a whale boat being seized in the jaws of an upside-down Sperm whale.

The Inuit traditionally hunted whales from small seal skin boats called umiaks. The arch made of whale ribs beside this umiak shows the size of the prey that could be taken from such small craft.

51

At some point, some extremely brave individuals showed that it was possible to actually overcome a live whale. Some whaling was practiced by the ancient Persians, Phoenicians, Vikings, Eskimos, and others. In subsistence societies, where one whale would feed a tribe for a long time, this probably did not pose much of a threat to populations. In Europe, however, where a cash economy had been created, hunters continued to kill whales long after local needs had been met because they could sell or trade the products to the outside world. Commercial whaling started there as early as the 11th century. As whale populations were destroyed, whalers moved on to new areas to continue hunting.

Right whales, which used to breed in many of the bays of Europe's Atlantic coast, were eliminated from one area after another. Eventually the Basque whalers, who started in Spain, had to go to North America to find whales. Except for a few stray individuals, the European population of Right whales is now virtually extinct, and the North American population is in very grave trouble. Somewhere along the way, the Atlantic Gray whale was completely destroyed, before a scientific description of the species, or even a drawing, was ever made.

Although we now consider whales to be "gentle giants" there are many reliable accounts of Sperm whales smashing and sinking whale boats, and occasionally even the larger ships that launched them!

IN 1320, in Britain, AN ACT of PARLIAMENT STATED THAT DOLPHINS, WHALES, PORPOISES and STURGEON WERE "ROYAL FISH" THAT COULD ONLY BE EATEN BY ROYALTY

The ancient Icelanders carved stirrups from whalebones.

An Inuit displays his catch. Whales furnished food, fuel, materials for clothing, housing, and tools—nearly all the necessities of life—for the Inuit of the far north.

Around the 17th century, the Dutch made the first of a number of technological "improvements" that spelled doom for whales. They developed the concept of processing whales at sea. Instead of bringing the whale back to shore to be utilized, the body was cut up aboard the ship and boiled down for oil. The meat, which was less valuable, was discarded. Before petroleum oil became widely available, whale oil was the fuel which was used in house and street lamps in all industrial countries, as well as for other purposes, including the production of soap, candles, cooking oil, paint, cosmetics, medicines, etc.

Improvements in ship building allowed whalers to go farther to sea, and to hunt open-water species such as Sperm whales, in addition to the slow-moving Gray and Right whales which breed close to shore, but were becoming rarer and rarer. Besides the oil that can be obtained from the blubber, Sperm whales have a great supply of very fine oil in the spermaceti organ in their heads. This oil is of such good quality that it was used to lubricate missile guidance systems and Swiss watches long after petroleum oil had replaced whale oil for most purposes. Scientists are still debating what use the Sperm whale itself makes of this vast store of semi-solid oil. Some believe that it is primarily an instrument to focus the whale's echolocation clicks into a narrow beam, while others have suggested that it is an organ of buoyancy, which aids the whale in making deep dives. Sperm whales also produce a mysterious substance called ambergris, which seems to be somehow formed from the indigestible beaks of squid that the whale has eaten. Despite the fact that it comes from the foul-smelling intestines of sick whales, ambergris has great value in the perfume industry due to its ability to "fix" an odor, so that a scent lasts much longer. At times it has been worth more than gold.

FIT FOR A KING! ALL WHALES CAUGHT WITHIN THE WATERS OF GREAT BRITAIN BELONG BY ANCIENT LAW TO THE CROWN— THE LAW PROVIDES THAT THE QUEEN MAY CLAIM THE HEAD, THE BODY GOES TO THE FINDER-- *AND THE TAIL TO PRINCE PHILIP*

Competition for Sperm whales' spermaceti— used to make candles—was so severe in 1761 that nine New England manufacturers agreed to evenly divide all whales within their territory and to fix the price of candles, thus creating America's first monopolistic trust.

top left—Sperm whale oil was both the finest fuel and the finest lubricant available at the beginning of the 20th century. These and its many other uses, made it one of the most essential commodities of the Industrial Revolution.

top right—Harpoon guns loaded with explosive-tipped harpoons, and mounted to large modern ships, removed much of the danger from whaling—for the whalers that is. They also made the outcome of the chase much more certain.

57

THE WHALEBONE SHED
Liverpool, England,
A LEAN-TO MADE ENTIRELY
OF WHALEBONE AND
USED FOR 100 YEARS

The tusk of a narwhal is sometimes 9 feet long and is the only naturally twisted object in nature that turns counter-clockwise.

Prior to the introduction of factory ships, much of the cutting-up of whales had to be done with the carcass still in the water—an extremely dangerous proposition in rough seas. This photo, taken over 100 years ago, shows a whale being "flensed," the process of stripping and peeling long strips of skin and blubber from the skeleton.

After the discovery of vast fields of petroleum oil in the early part of the 20th century, whale oil lost much of its commercial value. However, at about the same time, baleen became a very valuable commodity. It was used to produce a variety of products, including corsets, wigs, brooms, watch springs, umbrella ribs, fishing rods, brassieres, riding crops, shutters, trays, fans, etc. It was the "plastic" of the early 20th century. Baleen whales now became the main targets of the whalers. It is hard for us to imagine the killing of such magnificent animals to produce such mundane products, but people at that time believed that the ocean's resources were unlimited and had no idea of the intelligence of whales. Moreover, plastic had not yet been invented.

More technological advances doomed the remaining populations of whales. Great factory ships could process whales at sea around the clock while catcher ships continued to hunt them. Harpoon guns fired harpoons tipped with grenades or high voltage electrodes so that the whale could be killed without a fight. Whaling had formerly been extremely dangerous for both whale and whaler. Now the whalers had fewer risks. Air compressors were used to inject gas into the carcasses so they could not sink. Species of whales were added to the target list, which had previously not been killed because the bodies usually sank before they could be recovered. Faster boats meant that Blue and Fin whales, which used to outrun the whaling vessels, could no longer escape. As the great whales were killed off, the whalers even turned to whales that had formerly been considered too small to bother with, such as the Minke.

illions of whales were killed, and most of the great whales were reduced to only 5 – 10% of the original population size. In spite of scientific evidence showing that the level of take was too high to be sustained, species were not given protection until they reached the brink of extinction. Greed took precedence over rational management. In 1986 an international moratorium was finally declared on the taking of all the great whales. Nevertheless, some "pirate" whaling persists, and Japan and Norway continue to hunt Minke whales openly. Japan insists that its whaling is for "scientific" purposes, although all of the meat is sold. Both countries are lobbying to overturn the moratorium.

In addition some "subsistence" and "cultural" whaling is authorized for native peoples with a long history of whaling, including Inuit (Eskimos), people of the Caribbean Island of Bequia, and others. The latest group to receive approval for this type of whaling is the Makah Indian tribe of the Northwest coast of North America. They hunted whales for hundreds of years, but stopped for a long period until they received permission in 1998 to hunt Gray whales again. They killed their first whale in 1999. Even though the American Gray whale population has recovered, and has been taken off the endangered species list, the Makah hunt is controversial. The Makah insist that it is necessary to revive their culture and traditions, but anti-whaling activists claim that those traditions ended long ago and that the hunt is cruel and unfair to whales which have become accustomed to friendly contact with humans in whale-watching boats. The activists believe the hunt creates a precedent for other peoples to resume hunting, although they admit that the Makahs' quota of five whales per year poses no direct threat to the Gray whale population.

Combs used by natives of Tierra del Fuego, South America, are made from the jawbones of dolphins.

During World War II, whale meat was inexpensive and not subjected to rationing. After the war American military authorities attempted to ease the food shortages in Japan by encouraging the consumption of whale meat by the Japanese—most of who had never tasted whale meat before.

STEW
18 ¢
18

WHALE MEAT
Not Rationed

WHALE STEAK
Not Rationed

A Makah harpooner prepares to throw his weapon at a Gray whale off Washington State in May 1999.

Certainly, the economic importance of whale watching is greater than what has been realized by whaling. Around the world, wherever whales can be found with regularity, whale watching is a multi-million dollar business. Some people have become so passionate about whales and dolphins that they have even formed cults to worship them. Some of these believe that whales came to Earth from other planets to make contact with humans, or that dolphins can communicate telepathically with humans. Some conservationists believe that whale enthusiasts now pose a threat to whales and dolphins merely by giving them so much attention that they are unable to get about their daily business of feeding, resting, and mating. For this reason, whale watching is now regulated in many areas. In some places, feeding of wild dolphins has become an attraction. This practice has been shown to be harmful to the dolphins, and continues primarily because of the amount of money that is earned from visitors coming specifically for this purpose.

The number of people who view whales and dolphins in the wild is small, however, compared to the number that see dolphins and Orcas in marine parks. These attractions have also become controversial. Some people believe that humans have no right to keep other intelligent creatures in captivity for our own amusement. They claim that it is cruel to keep animals in an artificial environment where they cannot feed, travel, and socialize in a natural way, and that cetaceans are physically and emotionally harmed by being taken from their families, held in confined, unnatural conditions, and being forced to perform.

Those who support marine parks say that conditions and the level of care are much improved today over what they were in the past, and that most captive dolphins and Orcas can expect to live long and healthy lives. They say that captive cetaceans serve a valuable educational function, and that animals born or held for many years under human care are unlikely to survive if released back into the wild, as they have lost the necessary skills for survival.

THE **GATEWAY** of the Frisian Museum, in Wyk, Germany, IS MADE FROM THE JAWBONES OF A WHALE

For millions of people, marine stadium shows will be their only exposure to live whales and dolphins. Most people come away from these shows with an increased appreciation for the remarkable capabilities of these amazing animals.

A "friendly" Gray whale approache[s] a boatload of whale watchers in S[a] Ignacio Lagoon, Baja, Mexico. Ironically, when hunting was practiced in the Mexican breeding lagoons, the Gray whales defended their calves so ferociously that the whalers called them "Devilfish."

A blindfolded dolphin can distinguish a 2 inch diameter ball from a 2½ inch diameter ball from a distance of 5 feet!

The possibility of re-training captive cetaceans for life in the wild has been tested a few times with mixed results. The largest and most famous experiment is still ongoing. When the film *Free Willy* was released, the public was outraged to learn that the star of the film, an Orca whose "real" name is Keiko, was still being held in an under-sized pool in an amusement park under very unhealthy conditions. Keiko had several medical conditions related to poor care, and was not expected to survive much longer.

The film studio, conservation groups, corporate sponsors, philanthropists, and thousands of schoolchildren contributed to a fund to "Free Keiko." First Keiko was transported to a much larger facility in Oregon, where he received better medical care, learned to catch live fish, and got used to cold water again. His health improved dramatically. Then he was airlifted back to his native Iceland and placed in a large pen along the seashore where he can get used to the natural sounds of the ocean, including the calls of other Orcas, and be gradually weaned away from emotional dependence on his trainers.

Before Keiko can be released, however, he must show that he can catch enough fish to feed himself and demonstrate that he has all the skills he will need to survive in the wild. Most importantly, his trainers must be convinced that he will be accepted back into a pod of wild Orcas—hopefully the same pod from which he was originally captured. In captivity Keiko was able to substitute the attention of his trainers for the company of other Orcas, but in the wild, such a highly social animal is unlikely to do well without becoming part of a group.

Whether or not Keiko is finally released, and regardless of whether he survives in the wild or not, this massive effort to give a new life to one whale marks a milestone in the relationship between whales and humans. Instead of treating these complex and highly intelligent animals merely as sources of raw materials for our products we are showing that we can now respect them as species which have an equal right to share the planet, and to live their lives without our interference. The true test of this ethic will be to see if we can control the ever-increasing chemical dumping and pollution of the ocean, and the ever-increasing, large-scale commercial fisheries that kill cetaceans by entangling them in nets, and also depleting their food supply. In order to do this we will have to control our own numbers. The rapidly increasing population of human beings on the planet is leaving very little unpolluted natural habitat for wildlife, either on land, or in the ocean. The support shown for Keiko gives us hope that man and whales can exist together in harmony. If we can save the whales, we may just make the world a better place for ourselves and other creatures as well.

Keiko, the star of the movie Free Willy, *suffers from a droopy dorsal fin, a condition which occasionally occurs in wild Orcas, but is very common in captive Orcas—especially males.*

Interaction with fishing gear now threatens thousands of cetaceans annually, including this Humpback whale caught in a net off Newfoundland, Canada.

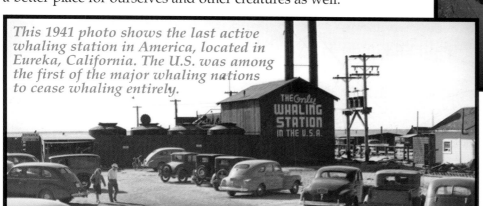

This 1941 photo shows the last active whaling station in America, located in Eureka, California. The U.S. was among the first of the major whaling nations to cease whaling entirely.

Glossary

Afterbirth– blood and tissue expelled from a female mammal during the birthing process. The afterbirth consists mostly of the tissues which connect the developing baby to its mother while it is inside her.

Ambergris– strong smelling substance found in Sperm whale intestines, particularly sick whales, valued for its commercial uses in the perfume industry.

Barnacle– a type of crustacean which usually lives inside a hard shell that it attaches to a rock, the hull of a ship, or some other object, such as the body of a whale.

Blubber– a layer of fat below the surface of a whale's skin, between the skin and the muscles.

Bubble-netting– elaborate feeding technique used by Humpback whales that involves the whale creating a funnel of air bubbles in which it entraps its prey.

Callosities– rough skin areas on Right whales. Callosities are normally infested with whale lice, which color them differently from the rest of the whale's skin. Scientists can use patterns of callosities to identify individual whales.

Cetaceans– the group of related animals commonly called, whales, dolphins and porpoises.

Cetologist– a scientist who studies cetaceans.

Convoluted– containing many twisted paths and sections.

Copepods– tiny planktonic (drifting) crustaceans which and are eaten by baleen whales.

Crustaceans– a group of animals with jointed legs and a hard outer skeleton, or shell, including lobsters, crabs, and shrimp.

Delphinidae– scientific name for the family of oceanic dolphins.

Diatom– a type of two-celled marine algae.

Dominance– a "pecking order," or social order that determines which animal gets the most power and priviliges.

Dorsal fin– the fin on the back of a marine animal. This is the uppermost fin—the one that sometimes sticks out of the water.

Echolocation– form of sonar used by toothed whales to locate their prey.

Endangered– refers to an animal population which is judged to be at great risk of going extinct.

Extinction– when all members of a species cease to exist.

Family– a classification of animals which may contain more than one similar genus.

Fetus– an alive, but as yet unborn baby still in its mother's womb.

Genus– scientific word for a group of animal or plant species that are related by evolution. A genus may contain one or more related species.

Hydrodynamic– moves easily through water with little resistance.

Imperiled– in danger.

Kraken– a Norwegian word for a legendary giant sea monster with long tentacles. Descriptions and drawings of the kraken seem to correspond with the giant squid.

Krill– small shrimp-like crustaceans which live in swarms and provide an important food source for whales.

Melon– an organ in the forehead of toothed whales believed to be used as a sort of "lens" to focus sound waves for echolocation.

Moratorium– a law or decree suspending or temporarily halting some activity.

Mysticetes– scientific name for the group of baleen whales.

Odontocetes– scientific name for the group of toothed whales.

Pectoral fins– the fins on the sides of marine animals, corresponding to our arms, sometimes called "flippers."

Phocoenidae– scientific name for the family of porpoises.

Plankton– marine organisms, usually microscopic, which drift with the currents, rather than traveling under their own power and direction.

Population– those members of a species which normally breed with each other, but not with other members outside of the population.

Pod– a group of cetaceans. This word is used like a "school" of fish, a "flock" of birds, etc.

Propulsion– a force that causes movement; a form of locomotion.

Rorquals– family of whales with expandable throat pleats.

Sonar– a device that is used to detect objects that cannot be seen with the eye. Sonar is an acronym for SOund Navigation And Ranging. It transmits sound signals and displays the echoes as a picture. It can be used to detect hazards to navigation (such as other ships at night or in a fog), to find fish, or measure the depth of water, to locate enemy submarines, or for many other purposes.

Species– a group of animals which are able to breed with each other, but not with members of other species.

Spermaceti– a semi-solid oil that was highly valued by whalers, contained in the spermaceti organ in the head of Sperm whales.

Testes– male sexual organs that produce sperm.

Tubercles– bumps found on the heads of Humpback whales. Their function is uncertain, but each tubercle has a small hair, which may act like a cat's whiskers to detect water motion.

Turbulence– disturbed or uneven motion in a fluid; the opposite of a smooth flow.

Index

A

Acoustic pictures-p.39
Acrobatic (habits)-p.26
Act of parliament-p.52
Ahab, Captain-p.2
Alaska-p.28, 34, 41, 43
Aluminum-p.40
Amazon River-p.35, 49
Amazon River dolphins p.25, 35
Ambassador dolphins-p.50
Ambergris-p.53
Ameland-p.51
America-p.10, 53
Amusement parks-p.57
Ancestors-p.3, 4, 9, 10, 11, 13, 24
"Anglo-Norse" (ship)-p.42
Animal husbandry-p.i
"Ann Alexander"(ship)-p.9
Antarctica-p.8, 25
Antelopes-p.10
Anti-whaling activists-p.55
Antlers-p.21
Apollo-p.48
Aquariums-p.i
Arctic-p.4, 25
Argentina-p.32
Aristotle-p.50, 51
Arm (human)-p.11
Art-p.48
Asia-p.10
Assault and battery-p.41
Atlantic Ocean-p.18, 19, 23, 28, 52
Atlantic Spotted dolphin-p.16
Atlantic White-sided dolphin-p.23
Attractions-p.56

B

Babies-p.3
Baby sitting-p.25
Bahamas-p.50
Baird's beaked whales-p.14, 21
Baja Peninsula-p.28
Baleen (whales)-p.13, 14, 15, 16, 17, 18, 19, 20, 27, 28, 29, 30, 36, 38, 40, 41, 47, 51, 54
Ball-p.56
Barnacles-p.19, 21, 28
Basque-p.52
Bats-p.39
Beached-p.47
Beak (dolphin)-p.35
Beak (squid)-p.23, 24, 53
Beaked whales-p.21, 36, 45
Behavior-p.16, 33, 42, 45, 46
Beiji-p.23, 24
Belugas-p.21, 35
(the) Bends-p.37
Bequia Island-p.55
Bering Sea-p.36
Bering Strait-p.49
Bible-p.49
"Big Bang" theory-p.45
Biology-p.16, 42
Birth (live)-p.2, 3, 12
Blackfish-p.23
Blind-p.24, 35
Blood flow-p.37
Blood vessels-p.7
Bloodstream-p.37
Blowhole-p.12, 17, 18, 20, 33, 46, 49, 50
Blubber-p.4, 9, 12, 27, 51, 53
Blue whale-p.7, 8, 9, 15, 19, 25, 30, 31, 39, 41, 54
Boats-p.9, 21, 23, 24, 26, 28, 34, 50, 55
Body-p.53, 54
Body heat-p.4, 9, 12
Body size-p.9
Body temperature-p.4
Body weight-p.12
Bones-p.3, 10, 12, 51
Bonnet-p.18, 29
Boto-p.35
Bottlenose dolphins-p.4, 15, 16, 22, 25, 33, 40, 41
Bouto-p.22, 35
Bowhead whale-p.14, 18
Brain-p.5, 6, 37
Brassieres-p.54
Brawls-p.27
Brazil-p.16, 50, 51
Breaching-p.26, 27
Bread-p.53
Breathing-p.3, 37, 46
Breeding-p.25, 27, 28, 29, 30, 43, 44
Bristles-p.4
Britain (see also "Great Britain")-p.52
British Columbia-p.32
Broadcast (radio)-p.i
Brooms-p.17, 54
Bryde's whale-p.15, 19, 30
Bubble netting-p.45
Bubbles-p.37, 41, 45
Buoyancy-p.9, 12, 53
Buoys-p.50
Burial grounds-p.51
Burial procession-p.51
Burmeister's porpoise-p.22
Butterfat-p.3

C

California-p.5, 8, 30, 34
Callosities-p.18, 29
Calves-p.3, 7, 8, 21, 28, 29, 33, 41
Campfire-p.49
Canada-p.44
"Canaries of the Sea" (see also "Belugas")-p.21
Candles-p.53
Captivity-p.33, 56, 57
Car-p.5
Carcasses-p.42, 54
Caribbean-p.55
Cartoon (whale)-p.i
Cats-p.2, 35
Cattle (see cow)
Cetaceans-p.2 (used throughout the book-other references not listed)
Chariot-p.48
Chemicals-p.38
Chin-p.4
China-p.35, 48
Clicks-p.25, 39, 45, 53
Climate-p.12
Coconut-p.5
Cold-blooded-p.4
Color (pattern)-p.32, 34, 46
Color perception-p.38
Combs-p.39, 55
Commercial fisheries-p.57
Commerson's dolphin-p.22
Common dolphin-p.22
Communicate-p.i, 26, 38, 39
Compass-p.40
Conservation-p. i
Conservationists-p.56, 57
Cook's Strait (New Zealand)-p.50
Copepods-p.18, 29, 30
Copper-p.40
Corsets-p.17, 54
Cosmetics-p.53
Cows-p.2, 3, 10
Crabs-p.34
Crustaceans-p.19
Cultural whaling-p.55
Cultures-p.48, 51, 55
Cults-p.56
Cuvier's beaked whales-p.15

D

Dall's porpoise-p.22, 24, 25, 34
Dances-p.49
Deer-p.21
Delphinidae-p.16, 22, 24
Dense-beaked whale-p.21
Diatoms-p.30
Dinosaurs-p.6, 7, 10
Dionysus-p.48
Disease-p.2, 40
Disguise-p.47
Divers-p.37, 50
Dogs-p.2, 40
Dolphins-p.i, 2, 5, 15, 16, 21, 22, 23, 24, 25, 31, 32, 36, 38, 39, 40, 41, 44, 48, 49, 50, 51, 52, 55, 56
Door-p.39
Dorado-p.16
Dorsal fins-p.18, 19, 20, 21, 23, 24, 25, 28, 32, 34, 35
Dutch-p.53
Dwarf sperm whale-p.20, 46, 47

E

Ears-p.11, 50
Earth-p.10, 12, 40, 56
Echoes-p.39
Echolocation-p.20, 25, 33, 35, 53
Educational function-p.56
Eggs-p.3, 6
Egypt-p.3, 10, 13
Elbows-p.11
Electrodes-p.54
Elephants-p.7, 10, 25
Embryo-p.17
Emotional state-p.39
Emotions-p.39
Endangered-p.18, 24, 29, 55
England-p.54
Energy-p.3, 12, 27
Engineers-p.36
England-p.21
Enviroment-p.24, 41
Equator-p.28, 32, 43
Eskimos-p.49, 52, 55
Europe-p.33, 46, 49, 52
Europeans-p.49
Evolution (see also "ancestors")-p.3, 46
Exercise-p.37
Explosive detonations-p.47
Extinct-p.5, 52
Extinction-p.10, 24, 28, 29, 30, 55
Eyes-p.24, 33, 34, 35, 38, 50

F

Face-p.28
Fat-p.4, 12, 27
Feeding-p.7, 19, 27, 28, 31, 33, 43, 45, 46, 56, 57
Feet–p.11
Fences-p.51
Fetus-p.4
Fighting-p.25
Fiji (an)-p.5, 45
Film (see also "movies")-p.2, 32, 57
Finger bones-p.11
Fingernails-p.13, 17
Fingers-p.11, 19, 20, 21
Finless porpoise-p.22
Fins-p.10, 18, 19, 20, 21, 23, 24, 25, 26, 28, 32, 34, 35
Fish-p.i, 3, 4, 5, 11, 13, 20, 24, 27, 31, 33, 34, 35, 38, 39, 40, 41, 45, 46, 47, 51, 52, 57
Fin whale-p.8, 15, 19, 30, 46, 54
Finback whale-p.46

G

Ganges River dolphin (susu)-p.22, 24
Germany-p.56
Gill cover-p.47
Gill nets-p.34
Gills-p.3
Gold-p.39, 53
Gods-p.48, 51
Gospel-p.49
Gravity-p.9
Gray Grampus-p.23
Gray whale-p.13, 14, 19, w25, 28, 29, 43, 52, 53, 55
Great Britain-(see also "Britain")-p.53
"Great fish"-p.49
Great White shark-p.31
Greece-p.48
Greek-p.48, 50, 51
Grenades-p.54
Gun-p.54

H

Habitat-p.42, 57
Habitat destruction-p.23
Hair-p.4, 17, 35
Hand-p.11
Harbor porpoise-p.22, 24, 33
Harpoon-p.5, 9, 18, 54
"Hashidate Maru" (ship)-p.19
Hats-p.49
Hatteras Inlet-p.50
"Hatteras Jack"-p.50
Hawaii-p.2, 43, 44
Heads-p.4, 11, 12, 18, 20, 25, 26, 28, 29, 30, 33, 35, 38, 40, 46, 53
Health-p.39, 56, 57
Hearing-p.11, 24, 38, 40
Hearse-p.51
Heart-p.7, 37
Heart rate-p.37
Heat loss-p.9
Hebrew-p.49
Heracles-p.48, 49
Herring-p.9, 32, 34, 41
Hector's dolphin-p.22, 23
Hips-p.11
Holland-p.5
Horses-p.2, 10, 49
Hourglass dolphin-p.22
Hudson River-p.26
Human fear-p.32
Humans-p.2, 4, 5, 16, 21, 23, 26, 28, 37, 40, 47, 50, 55, 56, 57
Humpback whales-p.2, 3, 4, 6, 12, 15, 16, 19, 25, 26, 27, 28, 29, 41, 43, 44, 45, 46
Humpbacked-p.26, 28

I

Ice-p.4
Ice cream stick-p.50
Iceland-p.57
Icelanders-p.52
India-p.10
Indo-Chinese-p.51
Indo-Pacific humpbacked dolphin-p.22, 23
Insects-p.19
Intelligence-p.i, 5, 56, 57
Internal structure-p.39
Intestines-p.6, 53
Inuit (see also "Eskimo")-p.5, 9, 12, 55
Iron-p.40
Irrawaddy dolphin-p.22
Island (Ka-y-ne)-p.49
Italy-p.38
Ivory-p.25, 45

J

Japan-p.34, 43, 44, 51, 55
Jawbones-p.51, 55, 56
Jaws-p.10, 11, 13, 18, 19, 20, 21, 32, 33, 45
Jet plane-p.39
"JoJo"-p.50
Jonah-p.i, 49
Jumping-p.i, 33
Jungle tribes-p.35

K

Ka-y-ne (Island of)-p.49
"Keiko"-p.i, 57
Killer whale-p.i, 13, 15, 16, 22, 23, 31
King-p.53
"Knuckles"-p.28
Kraken (see also "squid")-p.45
Krill-p.8, 18, 27, 30, 40

L

Lagoons-p.ii, 10, 11, 28
Lake Tung –Ting (China)-p.35
Lamps-p.53
Language-p.39
Law (see also "act of parliament")-p.5, 53
Legends-p.35, 48
Lice (whale)-p.18, 19, 28, 29
Life-jacket-p.12
Lifestyle-p.33
Liverpool (England)-p.54
London-p.21
Low frequency sounds (see also "moans," "sounds")-p.30, 38, 39, 40
Lunge-feeding-p.18, 41
Lungs-p.37

M

Mackerel-p.27
Magnetic field-p.40
Magnetic patterns-p.47
Magnetite-p.40
Mahimahi-p.16
Makah (Indians)-p.51, 55
Mammals-p.2, 3, 4, 5, 9, 10, 12, 13, 37, 38, 43, 50
Man-p.30
Maneuverability-p.26, 27
Manufacturers-p.53
Map-p.40
Marine biologists-p.i
Marine life-p.i
Marine parks-p.32, 56
Markings-p.47
Marriage-p.35
Mating-p.21, 25, 27, 29, 44, 56
Mauritania-p.51

M (cont.)

Meat (processing)-p.51, 53, 54, 55
Medical conditions-p.57
Medicine-p.51, 53
Melon-p.20, 21, 35
Melon-headed whale-p.16, 23
Melville, Herman-p.2, 3, 26
Mexico-p.24, 28, 43, 44
Mice-p.6, 10
Microphone-p.39
Middle Ages-p.49
Migration-p.2, 9,12, 27, 28, 29, 30, 43
Milk-p.3, 27, 41
Mimicry-p.47
Minke whale-p.15, 19, 54, 55
Missile (guidance system)-p.53
"Moby Dick"-p.i, 2, 25
Molars-p.35
Moans (see also "sounds")-p.38
Money-p.45, 51, 56
Monk-p.49
Monopolistic trust-p.53
Moose-p.21
Moratorium-p.55
Mountains-p.38
Mouth-p.17, 18, 29, 30, 41, 45
Movies-p.i, 33
Muktuk-p.12
Mullet-p.16
Museum-p.56
Music-p.44
Mustache (whale)-p.17
Myth-p.49, 50
Mythological tales-p.48
Mythology-p.49
Mysticetes-p.13, 14, 17

N

Names-p.16
Narwhal-p.i, 4, 15, 21, 49
Narwhal tusk-p.i, 21, 49
Nasal openings-p.17
Native Americans-p.48
Navigation-p.38, 40, 47
Neck-p.35
Netherlands-p.51
Nets-p.16, 21, 24, 34, 51, 57
New England-p.53
New York City-p.26, 46
New Zealand-p.23, 50
Newfoundland-p.21
Nitrogen-p.37
Nomadic-p.32
North America-p.28, 43, 52, 55
North Carolina-p.50
Northern minke-p.19
Northern right whale-p.18, 22, 29
Norway-p.32, 48, 55
Nose-p.4
Nostrils-p.11, 12
Nursery schools-p.41
Nursing-p.3, 7, 27

O

Oceanarium-p.i
Octopus-p.33
Odontocetes-p.13, 14, 17, 20
Odors-p.38
Odysseus-p.50
Odyssey-p.50
Oil (glands)-p.12, 18, 20, 36, 53, 54
Old Testament-p.49
"Opo"-p.50
Orcas-p.5, 6, 9, 13, 23, 25, 31, 32, 33, 34, 40, 46, 47, 48, 50, 56, 57
Oregon-p.57
Organisms (food)-p.13, 19
Organs-p.9, 11, 36, 38, 39, 53
Orinoco River-p.35

Otter-p.11
Oxygen-p.3, 37

P

Pacific Ocean-p.18, 19, 23, 28, 34, 42, 43, 44, 48
Pacific pilot whale-p.22
Pacific white-sided dolphin-p.23
Paint-p.53
Parasites-p.28, 47
Parliament-p.52
Peck, Gregory-p.2
Pectoral fin-p.11, 18, 19, 20, 25, 26, 32
"Pelorus Jack"-p.23, 50
Pelvic bone-p.11
Penguins-p.31
Performing-p.56
Perfume-p.53
Perrine, Doug-p.i
Persians-p.52
Petroleum-p.53, 54
Philanthropists-p.57
Phocoenidae-p.16, 24
Phoenicians-p.52
Photograph-p.24
Photographer-p.i, 22
Pilot whale-p.14, 16, 23
Pink river dolphin-(see also "Amazon River dolphin," "boto," "bouto")-p.35, 49
"Pirate" whaling-p.55
Plankton-p.25, 29, 38, 45
Plastic-p.17, 54
Pliny the Elder-p.50
Pods-p.25, 31, 40, 41, 50, 57
Poem-p.50
Polar regions-p.12, 32, 33, 43
Pollution-p.47, 57
Polynesia-p.51
Population-p.57
Porpoises-p.i, 2, 5, 15, 16, 24, 36, 50, 52
Porpoising-p.22, 36
Portugal-p.33
Poseidon-p.48
Predators-p.39, 47
Prehistoric (whale)-p.13
Prince-p.51
Prince Philip-p.53
Processing (meat)-p.53, 54

Products (whale)-p.52, 54, 57
Propulsion-p.11
Protein-p.3
Prozeuglodon-p.13
Pygmy beaked whale-p.21
Pygmy killer whale-p.23
Pygmy right whale-p.15
Pygmy sperm whale-p.20, 46, 47

Q

Queen-p.53

R

Radio-p.i, 44
Rays-p.31
Reefs-p.50
Reproduction-p.47
Researchers (see also "scientists")-p.26, 33
Ribs-p.49, 51
Ricks, Corena-p.i
Riding crops-p.54
Right whales-p.10, 15, 18, 19, 25, 29, 52, 53
Ring (wedding)-p.5
Ripley's Believe It or Not!-p.i
Ripley, Robert-p.i, ii
Risso's dolphin-p.22, 23
Rituals-p.51
River dolphins-p.16, 23, 24, 38, 49, 51
Rivers-p.24
Romans-p.50
Rome (Italy)-p.38, 48
"Roostertails"-p.34
Rorquals-p.19, 26, 28, 30
Rough-toothed dolphin-p.22
Royalty-p.51, 52
Russia-p.28

S

Sacred-p.51
Sailors-p.48, 49
Salmon-p.38
Salt water-p.30
San Ignacio (Lagoon)-p.28
Satellite transmitters-p.43

Scales-p.4, 19
Scars-p.21, 23
Scholars-p.49
Schoolchildren-p.57
Scientific description-p.52
Scientific observation-p.48
Scientists-p.i, 3, 10, 18, 19, 29, 30, 36, 38, 42, 44, 47, 50, 53
Scuba (divers)-p.37
Sea bass-p.49
Sea lions-p.31, 32
Sea of Cortez-p.24
Seaweed-p.21
Sei whale-p.14, 19, 30
Semen-p.29
Senses-p.38
Sensory organs-p.35
Sharks-p.31, 47, 49, 50
Shed-p.54
Sheep-p.10
Shellfish-p.18, 28, 35
Ship-p.5, 36, 50, 53, 54
Shipwreck-p.50
Shoehorns-p.17
Shoreline-p.47
Shoulder-p.11
Shrimp-p.8, 13, 30
Siberia-p.34
Sick (whale)-p.47, 53
Silver-p.39
Sinews-p.51
Singer-p.44
Singing-p.44, 45
Skeleton-p.10, 12, 21
Skin-p.4, 9, 12, 18, 20, 25, 30, 36
Skull-p.11, 24, 29
Skyhopping (see also "spyhopping")-p.38
Sleep-p.33
Snout-p.21, 24
Soap-p.53
Social bonds-p.40, 41, 47
Social groups-p.40, 57
Social life-p.5
Social status-p.38
Social structure-p.16, 25, 34, 41
Socialize-p.56
Sonar-p.20, 30, 33, 35, 38, 39
Song-p.44

Sound(s)-p.2, 11, 13, 21, 26, 30, 35, 38, 39, 40, 44
South America-p.35, 55
Southern minke-p.19
Southern right whale-p.4, 18, 29
Spain-p.52
Spectacled porpoise-p.22
Speed-p.9
Sperm (competition)-p.29
Sperm whales-p.5, 6, 15, 20, 25, 28, 36, 40, 45, 46, 51, 53
Spermatceti-p.20, 53
Spinner dolphin-p.22
Splash guard-p.17
Spotted dolphin-p.22
Spout-p.17
Spyhop (also see "skyhopping")-p.28
Squid (giant)-p.20, 25, 33, 34, 45, 53
St. Augustine (Florida)-p.i
St. Brendan-p.49
St. Matthew-p.49
Stick (ice cream)-p.50
Stirrups-p.52
Stomach-p.20, 45
Stories (see also "myths" and "legends")-p.50
"Stovebolt" knobs-p.28
Strandings-p.9, 47
Streamlined (bodies)-p.36
Striped dolphins-p.22
Students-p.i
Sturgeons-p.52
Submarine-p.2
"Sulfer-bottom" whales (see also Blue whales)-p.25
Super predators-p.13
Superstitions-p.35
Survive-p.56, 57
Swimmers (humans)-p.24, 50
Swimming-p.7, 9, 11, 12, 18, 27, 28, 30, 34, 36, 40, 43, 45, 47, 50
Swords-p.21
Symmetrical bodies-p.46

T

Taboos-p.35
Tadpole-p.30

Tags (identification tracking tags)-p.43
Tails-p.3, 11, 32, 33, 53
Talmud-p.49
Taste-p.38
Technological advancements-p.54
Technological improvements-p.53
Teeth-p.6, 13, 17, 20, 21, 22, 23, 24, 25, 34, 35, 45, 51
Telemachus-p.50
Television-p.22, 33
Temperature (body)-p.4
Temples-p.51
Throat creases (see also "throat grooves")-p.28, 29
Throat grooves-p.20, 21
Throat pleats-p.7, 18, 19, 28, 29, 30
Tiber River (Italy)-p.38
Tierra del Fuego-p.55
Tombstones-p.49
Tongue-p.6
Tooth-p.5, 6, 21
Toothed whales-p. 13, 14, 15, 16, 17, 20, 25, 38, 39, 40, 41, 47
Touch (sense of)-p.40
Trained (cetaceans)-p.33
Trainers-p.6, 57
Training-p.39
Transmitters (satellite)-p.43
Treasure-p.39
Treasure hunters-p.39
Tribes-p.35
Tropics-p.12, 25, 27, 28
Trucks (dump)-p.18
Tubercles-p.4, 26
Tucuxi-p.22
Turks & Caicos (Islands)-p.50
Turtles-p.31
Tusk (narwhal)-p.i, 21, 49

U

Ultrasonic signals-p.24
Umbrella (ribs)-p.17, 54
Underwater (diving)-p.36
Unicorn-p.i, 49
United States-p.i

V

Vancouver, British Columbia (Canada)-p.44
Vaquitas-p.24
Vietnam-p.51
Vikings-p.52
Vision-p.11, 38
Vitamins-p.3
Vocal cords-p.2, 44
Volcanic eruptions-p.47

W

Warm-blooded-p.4
Washington State-p.32, 51
Waste products-p.38
Watches-p.53, 54
Wax-p.20
Wean (ing)-p.41
Weapons-p.21
Weather-p.47
Webbed feet-p.11
Wedding ring-p.5
Weighed-p.19
Whale shark-p.49
Whale-two-headed-p.copyright page, i
Whale watching-p.26, 28, 43, 55, 56
Whaleboat-p.36
Whalebone-p.17, 52, 54
Whalers-p.4, 18, 20, 53, 54
Whaling-p.5, 19, 20, 28, 29, 51, 52, 54, 55
Whaling station-p.i
Whips-p.17
Whiskers-p.35
Whistles-p.39
White flag dolphin-p.22
White whale (see also "Moby Dick")-p.2, 21, 42
Wigs-p.17, 54
Windpipe-p.37
Women-p.49
World War I-p.50
Wrist-p.11
Wyk, Germany-p.56

Y

Yangtze River dolphin-p.23, 24
Yoga-p.37

Photo Credits

t=top   tl=top left   tr=top right
tm=top middle   m=middle   ml=middle left
mr=middle right   b=bottom   bl=bottom left
br= bottom right